How to Become a World-Class Manager

How to Become a World-Class Manager

Skills and insights for unleashing your leadership potential

Wayne Clarke

KoganPage

First published in Great Britain and the United States in 2023 by Kogan Page Limited

2nd Floor, 45 Gee Street	8 W 38th Street, Suite 902	4737/23 Ansari Road
London	New York, NY 10018	Daryaganj
EC1V 3RS	USA	New Delhi 110002
United Kingdom		India
www.koganpage.com		

© Wayne Clarke 2023

ISBNs

Hardback   9781398609723
Paperback   9781398609709
Ebook   9781398609716

British Library Cataloguing-in-Publication Data

A CIP record for this book is available from the British Library.

Library of Congress Control Number

2023931353

Typeset by Hong Kong FIVE Workshop
Print production managed by Jellyfish
Printed and bound by CPI Group (UK) Ltd, Croydon CR0 4YY
Kogan Page books are printed on paper from sustainable forests.

CONTENTS

LIST OF FIGURES AND TABLES

Figures

Tables

PREFACE

I was 26 years old and freaking out. I had recently moved from one of the Big 4 global accounting firms to work for a consulting business and my boss had promoted me to a managerial role. It was on a Friday and I spent all weekend worrying about what that meant. Come Monday, I was working with the exact same colleagues. But I was more senior. I had the flashy new title. I was meant to do things differently. And I'd had zero preparation for it.

This was my first glimpse of what it is to become a manager. Since then, I have discovered that virtually every other manager I have come across has been through a similar experience. In organizations across the world talented people are being promoted into management positions but are not being prepared for the real-life challenges they will face.

Yet training is a huge investment for organizations. In the United States alone, training expenditure was $92.3 billion in 2020–21, according to *Training Magazine*'s Industry Report. This is an average of $1,071 per learner. The average hours of training per employee were 63.9 hours per year. Meanwhile in the UK employers spent £42 billion on training in 2019, according to a recent government study – a spend of £2,540 per learner.[1]

There will always be an argument that employers should invest more in training, but, as the above data shows, it's not that they aren't dipping into the company coffers to 'tick the training box'. So why is it that bad management is costing employers £84 billion a year according to the Organization for Economic Co-operation and Development (OECD)?

Before I founded The Global Growth Institute, I had the good fortune to be managing partner of the advisory arm of Best Companies, which produced the Sunday Times Top 100 Companies lists. Over that time, I met hundreds of companies to talk about their challenges with employee engagement. Nearly all the chief executive officers, chief finance officers, chief HR officers and other c-suite officers talked about the middle manager. It wasn't always polite! They tended to blame middle managers for everything. Sales not at the level they wanted? It was the middle managers' fault. HR problems in the team? The middle managers were to blame. Customer feedback lower than expected? It's the middle managers, stupid.

It's true that manager behaviour has a big impact on staff performance. As my partner at The Global Growth Institute, Mark Vegh, wrote for The People Space: 'When bad management is common, staff turnover increases and recruitment costs rack up. Bad managers demotivate teams. This harms culture and productivity. Customers quickly notice and revenue is at risk. Ensuring managers get the support they need is not simply about being perceived as a 'good employer.' It's critical to business performance.'[2]

But our research at The Global Growth Institute has found that it is not all the fault of managers. Employers are too often setting managers up to fail. We surveyed 300 new and existing managers across the world in 2021 and discovered that two-thirds were excited about becoming a manager. But 62 per cent said they were not receiving the training they needed.

Even when organizations have put together what on the surface looks like a well-informed and well-intentioned management training programme, they too often fail to address the nitty-gritty challenges of what the realities of being a manager are like.

This is why we have taken the approach we have with our world-class manager training. We didn't want an academic model of what management today should look like. Instead, we wanted to offer practical and actionable tools to set you well on your way to being a truly 21st-century manager.

This book brings together the lessons we have learnt from observing great management over the years. It's a fresh take on what great management looks like; an instructional manual that every manager can pick up and make an impact within an hour.

And by picking up this book you are saying you don't want to just be any old manager. You want to be a world-class manager. I'm going to show you how.

Notes

1 Winterbotham, M, Kik, G, Selner, S and Whittaker, S (2020) Employer Skills Survey 2019: Summary report November 2020. assets.publishing.service.gov.uk/government/uploads/system/uploads/ attachment_data/file/936488/ESS_2019_Summary_Report_Nov2020. pdf (archived at perma.cc/8Y5Z-HF94)
2 Training Magazine (2021) 2021 Training Industry Report. trainingmag.com/2021-training-industry-report/ (archived at perma.cc/TG39-7YMU)
3 Vegh, M (2021) Managers Lack the Skills to Thrive. Here's How HR Can Help. www.thepeoplespace.com/ideas/articles/managers-lack-skills-thrive-heres-how-hr-can-help (archived at perma.cc/TA6T-RNH7)

Introduction

It was a cold day in Yorkshire in the north-east of England and I had travelled up from London to visit a contact centre to speak to a group of 60 managers. Before I started the session, the chief executive took me to one side and pointed out a particular manager. Let's call him Peter. It appeared that Peter was an outlier in this business. On every data set the business measured, from call handling to customer satisfaction, Peter was beating all the other managers. He was consistently the highest performer.

Now, this fascinated me. What was Peter doing that the other managers were not? When the session started I asked him if he would mind standing up and sharing what he did that worked so well. I realize now that this was not the best question, as people who are intrinsically good at doing something don't tend to know that they're really good at it. They are usually humble and don't think it's anything special. So, unsurprisingly, Peter just shrugged his shoulders.

I tried again. Could you talk us through what you do from Monday to Friday then, Peter? What does a great week look like for you when it comes to your team? Oh, he said, on Monday I spend most of the day going around the different contact centre pods and checking in with everyone, asking them how the previous week was for them and talking about the goals for this week.

That was his secret. The one thing he did that made him the top performer. He spent one day a week, 20 per cent of his working time, creating the space to focus completely on connecting and listening to his team members. The other managers could not understand this. Indeed, one of those present in the session put up his hand and said, so you only work four days a week then – prompting raucous laughter from all the others. These other managers viewed their role as primarily one of managing tasks. Peter saw it as managing people in addition to tasks.

Since then, my team and I at The Global Growth Institute have met hundreds of CEOs and thousands of great managers across the world, from Vietnam to Canada, from Mongolia to Germany, from New Zealand to Brazil, and asked a similar question. What is it that these world-class managers do that enables them to make a bigger impact than those around them?

It is this question that I address in this book but, before we start exploring the answer, it is worth taking a step back and explaining what I mean by a manager. So, for the purposes of this book, my definition of a manager is **anyone who has an impact on someone else's future in an organization.**

Now, most managers will have a team of people reporting directly to them. They will have their place on the traditional organizational chart with responsibility for x number of people. But organizations are changing. They are becoming less hierarchical. They are becoming more agile. The middle is hollowing out.

So my definition also includes those who may be a manager by title but who do not have an immediate team. These managers will have a range of internal stakeholders whose own opportunities to grow and progress will be impacted by the manager's behaviours, actions and results.

If that's the definition of a manager, then what is a world-class manager? It's a question I get asked time and again. And my simple answer is that a world-class manager is someone who other people say is a world-class manager.

If that sounds like a cop-out or somewhat subjective, just think back to those managers you have worked with who have inspired you to go that extra mile. That have motivated you. That have encouraged you. That have engendered a feeling of loyalty in you. That have enabled you to deliver superior performance and to be the best person you can be. I bet you can immediately think of a manager just like that. In your eyes that person is a world-class manager. It is subjective as far as the team member goes.

Let's go back to Peter. He wouldn't see himself as a world-class manager. But his team regard him as one. It is their experience of his management that defines him as exceptional.

So, in essence a world-class manager is defined by someone else's experience of your management. As David MacLeod, founder of the Engage for Success movement, replied when asked what great engagement looked like: 'It's when you see it.' So it is with managers – you know a world-class manager when you see and feel it.

Having said this, there are three key common traits in the world-class managers my colleagues and I have observed in the past 20 years (Figure 0.1):

- World-class managers behave like World-Class CEOs.

    o The world-class managers we have seen in action create value. They are dedicated to creating value for the organization and act as if it were truly their own. They demonstrate genuine care for people by spending time with them and actively listening to them.

    o We have also observed that exceptional managers have a sense of purpose and are focused on delivering on it. They don't accept mediocrity and will challenge in a supportive way to get the best from people. They focus on getting their operation to work extremely well for the benefit of the customer or end user. They are also very self-aware and want to improve themselves.

- World-class managers create highly engaged teams.

    o Getting clear on the team's purpose and helping everyone to work out what it means to them is our second essential. World-class managers make sure people are clear on what's expected of them, as nothing is more frustrating than not knowing what it takes to win. They measure the stuff that matters and don't bother with the stuff that doesn't. They also use their intuition.

Figure 0.1   Traits of a world-class manager

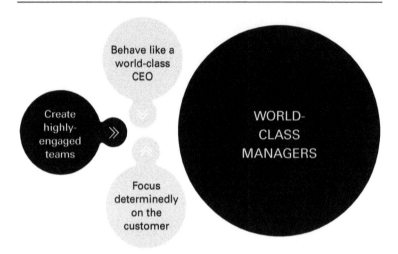

o A world-class manager acts as the bridge between what the leadership team and shareholders want and what those on the frontline want or need. Key to this is building strong relationships based on trust and delivering on what they say they're going to do, which is why integrity is quite often the most commonly used organizational value.

o Alongside this, great managers bring a sense of fun and enjoyment to what they do. We spend most of our lives at work and a key trait is knowing how to energize your teams.

• World-class managers are super-focused on the customer.

o The greatest managers take time to deeply understand what the customer wants now and are able to accurately predict what the customer will want next. A core trait is that these managers communicate exceptionally well. It sounds so basic, but poor communication is the biggest cause of frustration among people both inside and outside the organization.

o World-class managers work to align their teams, making sure each individual is clear about what their role is as well as understanding the wider role of the team. They share customer feedback, both good and bad, with their team in real time in order to help the team to be agile in reacting to what customer needs and wants.

Why do you need world-class managers in your organization?

As we travel around the world we speak to businesses, charities, non-governmental organizations (NGOs) and national and regional governments. And it is clear that most people understand that engaged teams serve customers better, generate more profit for companies and innovate more.

There's a substantial amount of research around this subject. Global analytics and advice firm Gallup has been tracking the impact of employee engagement on performance for decades. It has found that employees who are not engaged or who are actively disengaged cost the world $7.8 trillion in lost productivity. That's equal to 11 per cent of global GDP. According to its research, just 21 per cent of employees are engaged at work.

Those organizations with teams scoring in the top quartile on employee engagement saw the following benefits compared to those in the bottom quartile:

10 per cent higher customer loyalty/engagement

23 per cent higher profitability

18 per cent higher productivity (sales)

14 per cent higher productivity (production records and evaluations)

18 per cent lower turnover for high-turnover organizations (those with more than 40 per cent annualized turnover)

43 per cent lower turnover for low-turnover organizations (those with 40 per cent or lower annualized turnover)[1]

What Gallup research has also found is that it is managers more than any other factor that influence team engagement and performance. It's a compelling reason to want the best managers in your business for, according to Gallup, 70 per cent of the variance in team engagement is determined solely by the manager.[2]

The truth is that without world-class managers, organizations cannot deliver on the potential that exists in the form of you and the people in your team.

How to use this book

There are a plethora of management and leadership books out there – all of which offer their unique and useful perspectives. This book is not intended to compete with them. It is more journalistic and practical than theoretical. It is based on qualitative data, what I like to call an 'anthropological approach of observing managers in the wild'. From New Zealand to Brazil and everywhere in between, we have watched great managers in action and interviewed these managers, their colleagues and c-suite officers. From this qualitative data clear patterns and commonalities have emerged that we believe offer valuable insights on world-class management skills.

We have distilled this experience down into 12 pillars, which underpin our bite-size online training programme, World-Class Manager, which has been used for learning and development by more than 100 global organizations across the world. Some 30,000 managers have gone through the programme and received their World-Class Manager accreditation to date.

Now we have adapted these 12 steps into a book that is deliberately designed so that you can either read from start to finish for a comprehensive insight into management, or equally dip in and out of when you need to tackle a particular challenge. We know that training only works when you can put it into effect straight away. For example, if you were sent on appraisal training in February and don't need to do an appraisal until October, you will have likely lost the learning gained eight months earlier.

So, in each chapter you will find an overview of why that pillar is important if you are to become a world-class manager. We then outline the seven actionable steps to improve your performance in that area – what we call the WCM 7. We also pose some reflective questions to help you consolidate your learning. Plus, we include viewpoints from leaders throughout the book outlining what they expect from their managers and how they have dealt with the subjects we cover themselves.

Our goal is to better prepare you to succeed by helping you master the most important skills in day-to-day management. You may like to read this book cover-to-cover. However, we also hope you will pick up this book to learn or refresh yourself about the step you need at that particular point in your managerial life so that you can become, and continue to be, a world-class manager.

Notes

1 Gallup (2022). State of the Global Workplace: 2022 Report. www.gallup.com/workplace/349484/state-of-the-global-workplace.aspx (archived at perma.cc/Z4E2-FMMR)

2 Gallup (2015). State of the American Manager: Analytics and Advice for Leaders Report. www.gallup.com/services/182138/state-american-manager.aspx (archived at perma.cc/2RP8-FMP2)

01
How to be a 21st-century manager

Introduction

Managers are the lifeblood of every organization. I'm sure that, as you have picked this book up, you would agree with this statement. But if I asked you now to define what constitutes a manager and, indeed, management, I suspect we may not be in agreement. For being a manager isn't a static thing, though we often treat it as such. The concept of what being a manager is changes.

A quick delve into management literature finds there is no one agreement as to when management as a concept first arose. There are examples of management practice right back to the ancient world, but prior to the Industrial Revolution there was little in the way of what we would today recognize as 'modern' management practice. Business owners, rather than managers, handled most tasks such as planning, coordination and reward.

This all changed as organizations scaled up in light of the Industrial Revolution. To coordinate these larger factory-based organizations, owners needed to depend on others, those we today call 'managers'. These people focused wholly on areas such as workflow planning, standardized processes, quality control and labour specialization. Indeed, the first modern management theory is widely regarded as being based on American manufacturer Frederick Winslow Taylor's *Principles of Scientific Management* (1911) in which he argues that the principal object of management should be to secure the maximum prosperity for the employer, coupled with the maximum prosperity for each employee. To achieve this consistency, predictability and efficiency are tantamount. In other words, the system is the key and managers' role is to optimize the outputs.

Columbia Business School professor Rita Gunther McGrath argues that there are three ages of management since the Industrial Revolution, each emphasizing a different theme. This first phase, as outlined by Taylor, focused on execution, and is followed in the mid-20th century by a period of remarkable growth in theories of management, in which the emphasis is on expertise. It is during this time that we see the rise of management theory such as Six Sigma and objective setting, but this is also when influential business thinker Peter Drucker first coined the term 'knowledge work', in which value in a business is created by the use of information and the development of advanced services or products. Suddenly the manager role changed from command and control to motivation and engagement.

Gunther McGrath's final phase is what she calls the era of empathy. She describes it thus: 'If organizations existed in the execution era to create scale and in the expertise era to provide advanced services, today many are looking to organizations to create complete and meaningful experiences. I would argue that management has entered a new era of empathy.'[1]

In today's digital world, knowledge work has emerged as a critical element in many organizations. Gartner estimated that there were 1 billion knowledge workers in the world in 2019.[2] With the shift to remote work resulting from the COVID-19 pandemic, knowledge workers have become more important than ever, and the predicted rise in work automation thanks to artificial intelligence and other advanced technology is likely to make them even more important in years to come.

Knowledge workers think for a living rather than performing physical tasks. So, in the world of knowledge work we are trying to get the best from what sits in between someone's two ears – their brain. And the way to coax that out of someone, and get them to deliver their best, is through mutual respect, engagement and an understanding that your colleague wants to feel valued and listened to. This is what I believe Gunther is alluding to in her management era of empathy. And this is what makes a world-class manager.

Former IBM chief human resource officer Diane Gherson puts it this way: The role of the manager has changed so much over time that today a manager is a 'leader of people' rather than a 'leader of work'.

The job of a modern manager is challenging. They need to balance completing operational tasks with creating an environment in which people want to work. Increasingly the modern manager is all about the 'human touch'. We're in a world of individualism and personal brand where people want to express themselves. In such a world, getting the best from humans is where the party is. That's the essential skill of a 21st-century manager.

How do you do this? In this chapter we look at the seven steps you need to take and suggest some reflective questions to start you on this journey.

The WCM 7

- Think and act like a CEO.
- Be seen as a value creator.
- Create a stakeholder map.
- Engage your team – take them from good to great.
- Put the lens on you.
- Focus on the customer.
- Choose your attitude.

1. Think and act like a CEO

You may have heard of the famous NASA story. President JF Kennedy visited NASA and on his tour he asked a cleaner, 'What do you do?' The cleaner replied, 'I'm helping to put a man on the moon, Mr President.' It is a fantastic example of an employee being totally connected to their organization's vision and goal.

Every CEO in the world would love to create a total alignment of purpose in their organization, from the boardroom right to the frontline, where everyone is focused and energized to deliver the organization's vision and goals. Imagine if everyone in an organization were as engaged as this cleaner? What could that organization achieve?

As I mentioned in the Introduction, world-class managers think and act like a CEO. CEOs set the tone, vision and culture for their organizations. World-class managers ensure everything they do is underpinned by this vision and culture. They take accountability for their own and their team's actions, acting as if the organization were their own.

What is an organization's vision, mission and purpose?

The words vision, mission and purpose appear in many organizational statements, and it is easy to confuse them. The easiest way to understand these are as follows:

- Vision is the bigger picture. It describes what the organization aspires to be. It provides direction to everyone in the organization.

- Mission is what an organization does and for whom. It's sometimes described as the roadmap to get you to the vision. It can state the benefits provided by the organization.

- Purpose is the essence of the company. It is the organization's meaningful and enduring reason to exist, providing a call to

> action for the organization and a clear context for daily decision making. Purpose unifies and motivates stakeholders, especially employees and customers. You can't just talk about purpose; it needs to be felt.

Your role as a manager is key in getting alignment of your team with the purpose of the organization. Your ability to deliver on this will have huge benefits for your team, the organization and also for people personally.

What does it do for your team? It creates clarity of expectations, a real connection to the big picture and a feeling that what the team does really makes a difference. That's hugely motivational. For the organization it means that everyone is 'moving to the same drumbeat' as one CEO we worked with vividly described it.

Business educator and visiting lecturer Oleg Konovalov puts it succinctly in his book *The Vision Code*: 'No force is stronger than people united by a common vision; making decisions together and acting as one. Instilling a shared vision is a goal that precedes profit and is critical for the success of any organization.'[3]

To get into the mindset of a CEO, consider the type of behaviours they exhibit and apply them to your leadership.

Have clarity of vision

Take time with your team and make sure they are 100 per cent clear on the vision, on why it is important and how their role is crucial in helping to deliver it. Vision only becomes real when people know and understand it. Without this, everyone will be left to create their own definition of what success looks like and how they contribute to the business, which may be totally at odds with the strategy. You need to be crystal clear about where the company is going and be intentional and relentless about helping your teams to see that what they have achieved in work matters to you as a manager, to your organization and to your customers.

Be competitive

Many CEOs have big ambitions. Try thinking about how your organization could be the most successful in the market and what that looks like.

Stay positive

Positivity breeds positivity. We all have good and bad days, but you need to avoid complaining and find the positive aspect in any difficult or challenging situation. By amplifying positive energy and messages you can build a can-do attitude in the organization.

Be moral and ethical

CEOs do and say the right thing (most of the time). If you show your people that you live those values, others will follow.

Think before you speak

CEOs consider what they say, to whom and when. Consider the consequences of what you say or do and how you might be perceived.

Strive for improvement

Always try to think about ways that the organization and your team can improve, such as becoming more efficient, streamlined, profitable and with a more cohesive and engaged environment. Welcome feedback from your team on how they can contribute to this.

Set SMART goals

High-performing CEOs set themselves and the organization great goals. We discuss how to do this in the next chapter, 'Great goal setting'.

If every manager in your company executed these steps really well, then all your people might feel the same sense of connection as our NASA cleaner.

2. Be seen as a value creator

In simple terms, businesses create value through doing work to create a product or service, selling it to customers and capturing some of the value as profit. Creating sustainable value today is all about solving a unique problem or having a relevant point of difference. This has led some to say that value creation in the future will be based on the economies of creativity – be it the solution to a customer problem, the way a new service is sold and delivered, or personalization.

Managers create value by ensuring their team's contributions are improving the company's business. This can be through helping increase revenue, saving money, improving customer satisfaction or optimizing processes. In our work with leaders across the world we find that one of the most admired attributes is a manager who can create value – a manager who is proactive, driven and makes change happen.

To create value, it is vital that you are clear about the organization's strategy and what it means to you practically. Only then can you communicate this to your team. Our research with 975 global managers found that 71.9 per cent were clear about how their role impacts the strategy of the company and 76.5 per cent said they have opportunities to contribute their ideas.

World-class managers are not afraid to ask questions to ensure they have clarity about the strategy. If it isn't clear how you fit into the strategy, ask your leaders to explain it in simple terms. Only when you have this clarity can you set a vision for your team. Without clarity around a shared set of goals and why they are important, you will struggle to align your team.

Andrew Selley, chief executive officer UK at international food-service group Bidcorp, says he looks for managers who can add value to the triple bottom line – results, reputation and relationships. 'Finding ways of being more efficient, having more sensible ways of working but also finding things that could improve your service to the customer, reduce errors to the customer or ways to create greater employee engagement – these all add value to the business,' he says.

A willingness to learn, develop and upskill also adds value to your organization. Strong and positive working relationships with your customers, colleagues, peers and managers will demonstrate that you are a team player and show your positive intention in the organization.

Think about how you are adding value at the moment. Can you identify opportunities for you to do more?

3. Stakeholder mapping

World-class managers are great relationship builders with their teams, their customers and with those above them. They know that having great relationships can not only help them achieve their goals but will also enhance people's perceptions of them.

Take some time to test your relationship-building capability by first creating a stakeholder map. Figures 1.1 and 1.2 show examples of stakeholder maps. You can also find a blank template to fill in with your stakeholders at worldclassmanager.com.

Figure 1.1   Example of stakeholder mapping 1

Figure 1.2   Example of stakeholder mapping 2

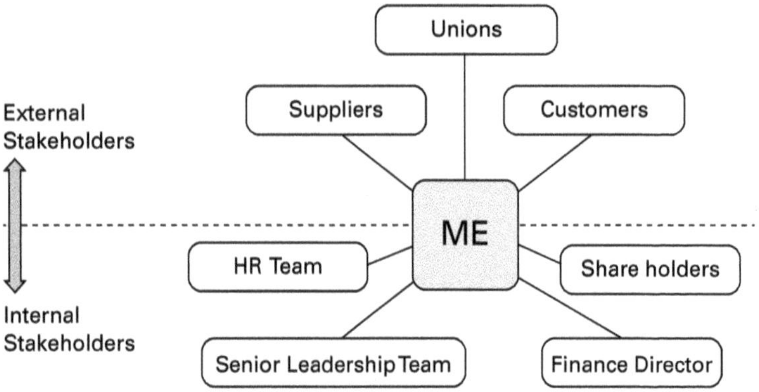

Now rate each of the relationships using a simple traffic light system of red, amber and green (with green being good and red bad). Think about how you've rated them – and why. When you reflect on this, what opportunities are there for you to enhance and improve any of these relationships, particularly the ones that you've marked red or amber? Think about how you might do that, and ask yourself what would ideal look like, to you and to your stakeholders. You can view a traffic light stakeholder map on our website worldclassmanager.com.

4. Engaging your team – from good to great

Employee experience relates to perceptions and feelings of workers towards their job experience, whereas employee engagement is about the perceptions and feelings of the employees towards their organization. Ensuring these elements are aligned and suitably prioritized requires a culture where leaders and managers alike put themselves in the employees' shoes.

DAVE MILLNER AND NADEEM KHAN,
INTRODUCTION TO PEOPLE ANALYTICS.[4]

World-class managers excel at engaging their people. They know that an engaged team will deliver that X-factor of discretionary effort which can move a team's performance from good to great. As we saw in this book's Introduction, 70 per cent of the variance in team engagement is determined solely by the manager.

So how good are you at engaging your people? It's time to be honest! Think about how your team would mark you out of five on the following statements:

- My manager shows care for me as an individual.
- My manager takes time to listen to my concerns and supports me wherever they can.
- My manager keeps me well informed of what's happening in the company.
- My manager helps me develop and achieve my potential.
- I am completely clear on what is expected of me.
- I am completely clear on how my role impacts the strategy of the company.
- My manager often thanks me and shows appreciation for my efforts.
- I have opportunities to contribute my ideas.
- My manager helps to create a positive, supportive atmosphere in my team.
- My manager is a great role model for me.

If you haven't achieved five out of five, check you are enacting the following steps.

Clear purpose

Being clear on the why, the purpose, is where great engagement starts. Ask yourself whether you communicate the company vision to your team on a regular basis. If not, consider how you can do this.

Active listening

Listening is a powerful tool for managers. But there is a big difference between merely 'hearing' someone and 'actively listening' to them. Hearing is passive. As the saying goes, the words someone is saying to you can go in one ear and out the other. Active listening requires your attention. If you are actively listening, you are showing you are genuinely interested in what the person is saying and want to make sure you understand what is being said. As leadership expert and author Steven Covey says, we should all listen with the intent to understand, not the intent to reply.

Developing your listening skills is essential for effective engagement. I particularly like how Karin Hurt, former executive of Verizon Wireless and CEO of Let's Grow Leaders, talks about building a culture of listening as essential to effective communication. She identifies three core elements of a listening culture:

- Tell the truth – nothing makes people tune out faster than smelling BS.
- Reward transparency – if you freak out every time you get bad news, people will fear delivering it.
- Encourage field trips – encourage cross-departmental or team visits.

Active listening requires suspending judgement. We will look more deeply at this in Chapter 4.

Solve their problems

Do you do what you say you will? Even fixing the most similar issue has a big impact on how your team views you. Combine this with active listening to ensure you are acting and solving things that matter to your people.

Increase recognition

Be intentional about looking for examples of the value your people have delivered and then plotting ways to regularly share them in the team and wider business.

Think about the weekly lived experience of your team

The experience we all have week by week is what shapes our opinion of the organization. The rise of the 'chief employee experience officer' in organizations is a testament to this. Map out your team's journey and make sure it's great. Think about 'a week in the life' of your team members. Walk through from start to finish for all of the different job roles and consider where there are elements that block them or where you can remove the friction.

5. Put the lens on you

Many great managers are very good at holding the mirror up to themselves. Building your self-awareness will enhance your impact. Think about the following questions:

- What is the current perception of you in your organization?
- Is it what you want it to be?
- Is it what it needs to be?
- Is there any difference between the two?

Now think about opportunity areas and where there is more that you could do to enhance the perception and the brand, both of yourself and of your team. Check out the questions for reflection at the end of this chapter. We will cover personal and team branding further in Chapter 12.

6. Customer focus

Customer satisfaction is a significant driver of the bottom-line performance of a company. The American Customer Satisfaction Index (ACSI) has conducted millions of interviews with US consumers regarding their experiences with major consumer goods and services companies and has found a positive financial impact for those with superior customer service, not only in revenue and profitability but also in stock returns. For example, the stock returns of those with excellent customer service as measured by ACSI had a return of 518 per cent between March 2000 and March 2014. Compare this to the S&P 500 – the index of the leading US publicly traded companies – which went up only 31 per cent over the same period of time.[5]

Managers can sometimes be removed from the customer, but it is by having a true customer service mindset and a relentless focus on delivering for your customers that you move from being a good manager to a world-class manager. Here are some ways you can do this:

- Know your customers better than they know themselves. By pre-empting their needs, you will service their requests before they even realize they need it.

- Profile your customer. Find out everything there is to know about your current and future ideal customers. What do they read? What issues are of interest to them? What social media channels do they most interact with? The more you know, the easy it is to market to them.

- Keep on the floor. As a manager you can often be removed from dealing with your customer unless something gets escalated to you, by which time the relationship your customer has with your organization can be damaged. Regularly interact and communicate with your customers to understand their needs and be able to adapt immediately when required.

We explore this more in Chapter 9.

7. Choose your attitude

We all have choices as human beings – and we can all choose our attitude at work. Being a manager in today's hectic world is pressured and very challenging at times, but the ability to manage ourselves and maintain a positive attitude in that 'pressure zone' is a key attribute of all the great managers we meet.

That's not to say that you can never show vulnerability, or perhaps even frustration at times (though make sure the latter doesn't take the form of inappropriate behaviour to your team, such as shouting or belittling). We are all human after all, and vulnerability is not being weak or submissive but rather shows you have the courage to be yourself. Indeed, a survey of more than 12,000 global employees by global non-profit organization Catalyst in 2021 found that employees are more willing to go the extra mile when their manager is open and shows vulnerability.[6]

However, maintaining a positive attitude is a key attribute of the world-class managers we have met. Great managers are great role models. People take their cue from them, so a manager's attitude, behaviour and communication will be very closely observed by their team and it will set the standard that the team will follow.

How would your team rate your ABC of Attitude, Behaviour and Communication, particularly when you are under pressure? Remember always to show care and understanding of your people, to be consistent and to use positive language.

Conclusion

In this chapter I have outlined seven traits that mark out world-class managers in the 21st century. In my conversations with CEOs across the world, these are what they look for in managers who want to develop to the next level. But world-class managers also need to be excellent in the execution of the day-to-day job they are doing too. It's no good being strategic if you are failing on the basics of your role. In the next chapter we look at one of the key skills a world-class manager needs to ensure they both deliver the best performance to the organization themselves as well as getting the best from their team – and that is effective goal setting.

Chapter review

Questions for reflection

As you consider your role as a world-class manager, reflect on the following questions and capture your answers in a way that works for you. Write notes, start a journal, record on your phone or capture on a spreadsheet – whichever will enable you to remember these points when dealing with your team and other people in your organization.

- How well do you support your team?
- How well do you communicate?
- And how well do you inspire your team?
- Take a moment to think about the things that make you feel great at work. What are they?
- Now think about your team… what would make them feel really great at work?
- What can you do to make that happen?

Actions to take now

- Test your vision for your team. Does it motivate you and your team? Is it aligned to the vision and strategy of the organization?
- Map your stakeholders. Assess all your key relationships (traffic light style – red, amber, green) and highlight any opportunity areas to improve them. Assess how your stakeholders see your team? Are your team creating the necessary impact and perception or could you enhance it? How could you do that?
- Seek feedback on your personal impact; act on any opportunity areas highlighted. Create an evaluation and review process and commit to continuous improvement and development.

Notes

1 Gunther McGrath, R (2014) Management's Three Eras: A brief history. hbr.org/2014/07/managements-three-eras-a-brief-history (archived at perma.cc/EZB3-C6C8)

2 Roth, C (2019) 2019: When We Exceeded 1 Billion Knowledge Workers. blogs.gartner.com/craig-roth/2019/12/11/2019-exceeded-1-billion-knowledge-workers/#:~:text=At%20some%20point%20this%20year,many%20knowledge%20workers%20in%20history (archived at perma.cc/SDB8-MPEX)

3 Konovalov, O (2021) *The Vision Code: How to create and execute a compelling vision for your business.* Wiley, Hoboken, NJ

4 Millner, D and Khan, N (2020) *Introduction to People Analytics: A practical guide to data driven HR.* Kogan Page, London

5 ACSI (2020) An Interview with Claes Fornell, Founder and CEO of the American Customer Satisfaction Index ACSI. www.theacsi.org/news-and-resources/insights/2020/06/15/an-interview-with-claes-fornell-founder-and-ceo-of-the-american-customer-satisfaction-index-acsi-2/ (archived at perma.cc/P8NJ-AND8)

02
Great goal setting

Introduction

Goal setting is about helping you to succeed by creating energizing milestones en route to achieve your goal. That might be a specific project-based goal, a bigger strategic goal or a goal around an aspect of personal growth. The point is that people who clearly articulate goals are more likely to achieve them.

Research shows that setting specific difficult goals yields considerably higher group performance compared to non-specific goals.[1] Goal setting is connected with self-confidence, motivation and autonomy according to goal-setting pioneers Locke and Latham.[2]

According to Amy Gallo, author and contributing editor to *Harvard Business Review*: 'Helping employees set and reach goals is a critical part of every manager's job. Employees want to see how their work contributes to larger corporate objectives, and setting the right targets makes this connection explicit for them, and for you as their manager.'[3]

World-class managers excel at goal setting. That doesn't have to mean sitting there with a pen and paper and writing goals, though research finds this increases the likelihood of success, as we will see later. It could just be that you talk through your goals with someone, thereby ensuring some accountability for delivering on those goals. Or you can use visualization techniques, basically picturing what success looks like.

The effectiveness of visualization is backed by research. A famous study at Cleveland Clinic Foundation in Ohio compared results of people doing physical exercises with those who did virtual exercise in their heads and measured this through finger abduction, basically spreading your fingers. Those who did the physical workout increased their finger abduction strength by 53 per cent. Those who visualized it through 'mental contractions' increased their strength by 35 per cent. What was most interesting, however, was that the visualization technique had long-term impact, with those who had used it having a 40 per cent increased gain four weeks later.[3]

Goals can be explicit (or specific). They can be a vision, a painted picture of a future reality. They can be a feeling you have about where you want to get to. Not everything has to be linear. But again, one thing is for sure: the more effort we can put into articulating these key milestones, the more likely they are to be achieved.

World-class managers are focused on getting the best out of themselves and the best out of others. Focusing on your own goals is as important as those of the people who depend on you for support and inspiration. Your ability to understand, and where possible support, the delivery of their goals is vital to building your relationship with key stakeholders inside and outside the organization.

Most people are pretty effective at hitting targets and goals if they are easy to understand. But most people don't take the time to set any clear goals. It's one thing setting a goal, another to have a plan to execute it. World-class managers set clear goals, articulate a plan for achieving them – building in some flexibility – and ensure there are sufficient resources to achieve the goals. In doing so they win for their teams and themselves. Here's how.

The WCM 7

- Create a vision for success.
- Provide context and use positive language.

- Get SMART.
- Break the goal down into small steps.
- Write goals down and review them regularly.
- Balance goal setting between the individual and the business.
- Recognize and celebrate success.

1. Create a vision of success

We need to have a clear idea of what success will look like, otherwise how do we know what we are aiming for or that we have achieved it? Success is subjective, so if we don't have clarity around it, people will revert to their personal idea of what success is. Success can be defined as a favourable or desired outcome. It may be a quantitative measure such as increasing customer conversion rates by a certain percentage or responding to internal enquiries within an hour. It may be improving customer perceptions of your brand or fixing customer problems.

Whatever it is, world-class managers clearly articulate what success looks like and make it something energizing. Fixing customer problems is not very exciting. But improving someone's life is.

Use the framework shown in Figure 2.1 to create your vision of success.

Figure 2.1   Creating a vision of success

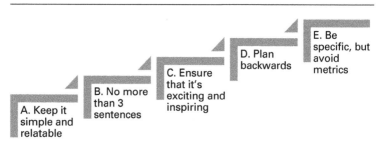

A Start thinking of relevant words to describe what success looks like. Write down whatever comes to mind and start to pick out the words that are most relevant and understandable for you and your team. Once you have the most relatable and inspiring words, think about how these can create what success looks like for you.

B Ideally you would want to keep your vision to three sentences or fewer, otherwise it will not be a memorable and relatable vision for others to grasp.

C Always use positive and aspirational words. You want to stretch what you think is possible for it to be truly exciting and inspiring.

D Once you know what you want your future to look like, you can plan for the present by asking yourself what needs to change and how you can achieve this change. List the things in your future that you don't have in your present. Then work out what needs to change to ensure that you fulfil the vision for the future.

E Draft out your vision and review with your team. Tweak and amend anything that does not fit or inspire. Highlight the parts that do feel inspiring and accurate. The vision needs to produce a mental image when read and uses positive, emotive language.

An organization can lose sight of its vision and instead focus strictly on the metrics. So, avoid using metrics, such as 'we will increase sales by 20 per cent over the next five years'. This is not inspiring for you or your team. Describing how the future will look, and how the organization hopes to achieve it, is.

2. Provide context and use positive language

Helping your team understand **how** and **why** their role is important and how it connects to the vision is crucial. It creates alignment to the organization's purpose and helps people see that they have an important role to play. Providing this context to your team is helpful before you drill down to the individual goals. A great tip here is to be aware of your language when doing this. Use positive language to describe and frame your goals. Often in our daily lives we use negative language filled with don'ts and can'ts. 'I don't have time to exercise.' 'I can't write that article.' Make sure you talk about what you do want to do rather than what you don't want to do to get everyone engaged in the goal.

3. Use the SMART goal-setting model

There are a number of models to help you set goals, but we suggest that a simple and easy-to-use framework to start with is the SMART model:

S is for Specific. It asks, is your goal specific or is it merely a vague, simple goal? Is it well defined, unambiguous and clear? If you know exactly what you want to achieve, you know where to concentrate your efforts and you can avoid distraction.

M is for Measurable. As the old saying goes, you can't achieve what you can't measure. Make sure to create good measurement and monitoring criteria for your goals – whether they are numerical targets, customer or employee satisfaction figures or any relevant target that will help you assess how you are progressing.

A is for Attainable. Is the goal attainable based on an individual's or team's ability or their current workload and whatever else is going on in the business? Are you being realistic in what you think is actually possible and what people can realistically commit to? Can you actually meet the expectations you have set? If you set the bar at the right level, you will achieve a healthy degree of stretch that will energize and focus the team towards the goal. Setting the bar too high can lead to frustration and disengagement, so do make sure you get the balance right. Stretch is good, stress is bad.

R is for Relevant. Are your goals and your day-to-day activities relevant to help you achieve the vision and strategy of the organization, to meet your stakeholders' needs or to fulfil the ambitions of your team members? Constantly monitoring your goals and making any necessary adjustments is important to keep you on track and keep activity relevant.

T is for Time-bound. As American author Napoleon Hill once said: 'A goal without a deadline is just a dream.' There must be a deadline to achieve your goal.

Let's see what that would look like in practice. Say you want to publish a book. A simple goal would just be to say, I'd like to write a book. Now let's make that into a SMART goal.

S: I want to write a book on world-class management (not just management).

M: I will write a chapter of 3,000 words every week to get to 50,000 words in total.

A: I run a business based on world-class management so I have the experience and basic outline in my head already.

R: By writing the book I will be able to use extracts to promote my business in publications, on social media and on our website.

T: The book will be published in March 2023.

Now, SMART on its own won't make all your dreams come true, but having a clear timeframe and endpoint will provide energy and focus. It is also a great way to hold yourself accountable.

4. Break the goal down into small steps

Athletes and sports people know that if you want to run a faster time or jump a greater distance, you don't try to achieve the new target in one big leap – you break down your target into smaller steps and work towards it over a period of time. And it's the same principle with any goal.

Why is this?

- Well, first, small steps are not overwhelming, meaning you are more likely to take these steps. They are attainable.

- Small steps propel you forward, helping you to establish habits and see that you are progressing.

- Small steps make it easier to keep going as you increase in confidence and motivation. Success breeds success.

- Small steps taken together add up to a big result. Just think about sales calls. If you set a goal to make 30 calls a day, by the end of a month you will have nearly 700 calls. This is a more manageable goal to set a team member than 'make 700 calls this month'. It is a bit like the answer to the old question – 'what's the best way to eat an elephant?... One bite at a time.'

5. Write down goals and review them regularly

Writing down your goals and reviewing them regularly has been shown to improve the chances of success by a significant amount.

A study by Dominican University in California researched 267 participants from a wide variety of businesses, organizations and networking groups in the United States and overseas to discover how goal achievement in the workplace is influenced by writing goals, committing to goal-directed actions and accountability for those actions. Psychology professor Dr Gain Matthews found that more than 70 per cent of the participants who sent weekly updates to a friend had completely accomplished their goal or were more than halfway there, while only 35 per cent of those who kept their goals to themselves, without writing them down, were at the same stage.

World-class managers review their goals **at least once a week**. If you don't think about your goals, you won't make them happen. If you are not reviewing what you are doing relating to your goals, then they are just a pipe dream that will never be achieved.

Plan – Do – Review – this should become your goal-setting mantra.

6. Balance goal setting between the individual and the business

Goal setting needs to be good for the individual as well as good for the business. It should not favour one at the expense of the other. World-class managers get this balance right.

One way they do this is by understanding the motivators for both the business and the individual when building goals. People are much more motivated by activity that has a personal benefit to them and that they enjoy and find meaningful. Ask your team members what they are personally trying to accomplish and see if you can feed that into the goal. But don't forget these goals still need to fit into the overall mission of the organization.

Another is to give your team members ownership over their individual goals. Ask them to start by drafting their own goals, remembering to show how they feed into the organization's strategy. You can then sit down with the team member and discuss whether the goals are SMART and also whether they 'stretch' that individual. In other words, are they challenging enough for that team member? By having a voice in setting their goals, people will feel more accountable for hitting them.

You and your team should regularly come together to review and agree on individual and team goals and how they align to the organizational goal. During the goal-setting review sessions, you will need to give your people the time and space to reflect on where they are, what the team has achieved and where it wants to go. In the reflection session you should review areas of underperformance or misunderstanding and highlight anything that blocks success in achieving the goal, such as lack of support or resources.

These goal-review sessions for the individual and the team will allow everyone to feel more involved and bought-into the goals. In turn they will feel that their contribution is valuable and hopefully focus on how to achieve the required results.

7. Recognize, thank and celebrate successes along the way

This is a step that is often neglected by less-effective managers. Recognition is vital for motivation: people love to see that they are making progress and are having a positive impact. By celebrating successes, however small, you are helping to reinforce the motivation required to move on to the next achievement.

World-class managers are brilliant at giving recognition. They not only thank people but, crucially, they help them to see the impact of their efforts on the business, on the team, on customers and on all their stakeholders. Every member of your team should be able to put into words exactly how their efforts contribute to the company strategy.

Making people aware of the impact of their work is even more powerful than simply saying thank you. People want to find meaning in their work and to be inspired. When they see this, they are more engaged and productive.

Here are some simple ways to recognize, thank and celebrate your team successes.

Share customer feedback publicly

Your people will feel engaged with the outcome of their work when they hear about the positive comments from your customers. Sharing this feedback with your team's colleagues/peers and your own manager will celebrate their hard work and contribution.

Share personal achievements

By creating space for personal accomplishments and hobbies within the workplace, you'll be recognizing your employees as the multifaceted individuals they are.

Weekly success meetings

These sessions are a perfect opportunity to share your team's individual and group successes. By holding them regularly, your people will get to hear how what they contribute has had a positive effect on the company.

Send a note with specifics

Sending a note to one of your team personally has a bigger impact than you think, especially when you specify exactly what your team member has done and the impact of their actions.

Offering wellbeing or therapies

Offering the chance for your people to take time out from their duties during their working hours to take part in, say, a yoga session or access to a counsellor will instantly make them feel like you care for them as an individual and for their mental and physical wellbeing.

Team lunch

Celebrate success or recognize a job well done by hosting a team lunch. During the lunch you should highlight what or who the celebration is for and what has been achieved.

Let your manager know what has been achieved

It is important for you to recognize and reward your people, but it has even more impact when you inform your own manager so they can acknowledge the achievement. This provides a massive boost to your people, knowing that they are being recognized higher up in the organization.

Offer time back

Offering to give your people some precious time back is a great way to show your appreciation for their efforts. For example, allow them to leave an hour early to reward them for their hard work.

Share the positive news

Using social media is a great way to amplify your team's successes and achievements. Platforms such as LinkedIn, Twitter, Instagram or your company intranet or other communication channel like Slack are the perfect way to amplify your good news stories.

Make sure recognition is one of the top items on your manager checklist.

Conclusion

Effectively setting goals is one of the main skills of a world-class manager. If you can't do this, all else fails. Goals help you and your team to focus on the right actions as well as helping to trigger new behaviours and maintain momentum. Without goals it is difficult to measure progress.

Goal setting seems so simple but, in reality, many people find it hard to develop relevant, clearly defined goals for themselves and their teams. All too often we can find our goals are vague and do not keep us accountable. So, work through the WCM 7 to ensure your goals are unambiguous, achievable and that there is a clearly defined pathway to achieving them. Being a great goal setter will make life all the easier when it comes to the dreaded appraisal, which we discuss in the next chapter.

Chapter review

Questions for reflection

As you consider your role as a world-class manager, reflect on the following questions and capture them in a way that works for you. Write notes, start a journal, record on your phone or capture on a spreadsheet – whichever will enable you to remember these points when dealing with your team and other people in your organization.

- How well have you and your team articulated your vision and definition of success?
- Is everyone clear on the vision, and on their role in helping to deliver it?
- Is it something that excites and energizes you all?
- Does it align to the goals of your organization?

Actions to take now

- Review your own goals. Are they aligned to the organization's purpose, mission and strategic goals? Are they specific, SMART goals? Is the team clear on its roles in delivering them?
- Sit down with your team and ask yourselves, what do we want to be famous for?
- Have fun. Goal setting should be fun. If it isn't, maybe you're not setting the right goals. You should be excited by your goals – if you are not, then something isn't right. Review your goals and strengthen them so they make you excited.

Notes

1   Kleingeld, A, van Mierlo, H and Arends, L (2011) The Effect of Goal Setting on Group Performance: A meta-analysis. *Journal of Applied Psychology*, 96(6), 1289–304

2   Locke, E and Latham, G (1991) A Theory of Goal Setting & Task Performance. www.researchgate.net/publication/232501090_A_Theory_of_Goal_Setting_Task_Performance (archived at perma.cc/ M4BN-YLV4)

3   Gallo, A (2011) Making Sure Your Employees Succeed. hbr.org/2011/02/making-sure-your-employees-suc (archived at perma.cc/83LJ-X3BJ)

4   Gardner, S and Albee, D (2015) Study Focuses on Strategies for Achieving Goals, Resolutions. Dominican University of California.

scholar.dominican.edu/cgi/viewcontent.cgi?article=1265
&context=news-releases (archived at perma.cc/W2JD-HNFS)

5 Ranganathan et al (2004) From Mental Power to Muscle Power
– Gaining Strength by Using the Mind. pubmed.ncbi.nlm.nih.
gov/14998709/ (archived at perma.cc/N66Q-7XL8)

03
View from the top: 21st-century leadership

A bit of skill and a bit of luck. That's how Andrew Selley describes his career.

Starting as a graduate trainee in a company that distributed Pepsi, within three months the business had moved to distributing Coca-Cola, effectively quadrupling its size and, in a stroke of luck, immediately providing Andrew with more opportunities. He quickly moved around the business, covering national supply chains, sales, national accounts and marketing before ending up as trading director in its wholesale channel 10 years later.

After being headhunted to join a company in financial trouble, he found himself once more in a larger group when the business was acquired – again providing new opportunities for his career. Fast forward two decades and after a journey that takes in running logistics supplies to high street names KFC, Nando's and Pizza Hut, supplying food to armed forces across the world, setting up a Middle East business and overseeing the Baltics operation, Andrew now heads the UK division of international foodservice group Bidcorp.

Bidcorp at a glance

In the UK, Bidcorp employs 7,000 people and has a turnover of some £2 billion. It comprises Bidfood, which supplies food, drink and packaging to hospitality – from restaurants and hotels to schools, hospitals and prisons – plus a fresh and frozen fish business, fresh fruit and vegetables and a fresh meat operation. Then there are a couple of manufacturing businesses and other independent wholesale firms. All are focused on the hospitality sector. The global company, listed on the South African stock exchange, operates in 35 countries and is run as a decentralized group with best practices widely shared.

Of course, without skill Andrew would not have succeeded in all these jobs and, thanks to the range of roles he has undertaken throughout his career, he now brings wide experience to his position as chief executive. So, he has a clear view about how managers can add value to his business today. He explains:

> We operate what we call the triple bottom line: results, reputation and relationships. So it is about financial results. But it's also about our reputation – our service to our customers – which gives us longevity and the ability to potentially command higher prices. And it's also about relationships – employee engagement, customer relationships and so on. So, if a manager can give us ways to improve in any of those areas, that's value. As a manager you are coming into work every day and can see things which seem really stupid and it's your responsibility to ask, why are we doing this? Is there a different way of doing it? As CEO I would never notice these as they are not visible to me every day. So, finding ways of being more efficient, having more sensible ways of working, but then also finding things that could improve your service to the customer, reduce errors to the customer or ways that will create greater employee engagement – any of these areas where a manager can add value are equally valuable to us. If you want to progress in your career, then you have to be able

to demonstrate that you are adding extra value and thinking about things differently.

However, he cautions that you cannot do this without first being great at the day-to-day job.

> I would often go to my boss and say, here's an idea of how to
> do something differently, or we could try this and do that. But
> fundamentally if I've got somebody who's not delivering results but
> just keeps coming and telling me how we could do things differently
> then I'll probably just think you're not actually focused on what
> you're meant to be doing. So the first thing is you have got to do
> brilliantly what you do.

While Andrew believes being strategic is important, he says that the speed of change in the world means reactivity, adaptability and flexibility are just as valuable today. For example, his pre-pandemic strategy was ripped to pieces when COVID-19 appeared. Business went down 80 per cent in a week. The ability to react and change speedily in response to that was vital for survival.

As CEO, the decisions Andrew takes affect his employees' livelihoods and much time is spent engaging stakeholders – suppliers, customers, banks, the community and employees. There's an element of responsibility and accountability that comes with this that world-class managers should look to develop if they want to progress, as we outlined in Chapter 1. As Andrew has been in the business for a long time, he says he has built relationships over time so that it has become a natural part of communication rather than a planned emphasis of engagement. He adds:

> But if I were starting from fresh then my process would be to
> spend time speaking to the stakeholders and asking what it is that
> is important to them and really understanding what the important
> results and outcomes are to each individual stakeholder. Then making
> sure that I understand how they measure whether it's a good or bad
> outcome in the area that they're interested in. And then you work
> out your plans to deliver the good outcomes and you make sure you
> are communicating those good outcomes and reminding them that,

if I remember rightly, Siân, you said you were interested in this and a good outcome would be that. And by the way, we've delivered that but we've got a few problems in delivering this, so if you could help us in this, that would be really helpful. So that is how you would do it from scratch.

Having worked in many roles in the business himself, Andrew is keen that the senior executive team keeps grounded. One way this has been done is through 'street teams' – an initiative where all of the senior management team had to get 'back to the floor', working on a day shift, night shift, with the freezer team and so on. 'It's so we don't lose track of reality. When you are at a senior level you do spend much of your time working with industry bodies, trying to influence government strategy, working with the banks, with shareholders, and you can forget that what your job is about is picking and delivering food to restaurants. Therefore, it's important to make sure you are grounded in this.'

It helps that Bidcorp UK's head office and support functions are mainly spread out among the depots rather than in a head office. It's a decentralized, empowered business with a global CEO who lives in Australia to whom Andrew speaks once a month.

Much of our internal communication and engagement is about encouraging our managers and our leaders of depots and departments to be decentralized, to do their own thing as long as they deliver the results. We have some national customers that we've got agreements with whereby we have to do the same, whether that's in Scotland or Kent, so there are certain things that are non-negotiable, but much of our time is spent encouraging people to express their individualism and do things their own way.

So, from that context, engaging people is more about the continual painting of the picture of where we want to be as a business, what the vision is for the business and what our values are. So it's continual re-engagement with the values, continual re-emphasis of the vision, continual reminders of the fact that we're focused on the triple bottom line. So it's not profit at any cost. It's about having great service and great, engaged employees that will deliver the numbers.

One big change over Andrew's career has been the erosion of trust in institutions. This means there has to be more collective acceptance than in the past, he says. 'The days of the older CEO in bowler hat coming out and barking some dictum, which got typed up and stuck on a memo board and everybody had to do it, they don't exist any more, thankfully.' In light of this, he says, today's CEOs and managers have to spend more time in considering different options, engaging and communicating with all stakeholders.

Fundamentally, however, Andrew says the 21st-century CEO and 21st-century manager share the same objective.

'Whether it be my first job as night shift manager in a Warrington warehouse to now that I'm CEO of Bidcorp UK, the results are different, the numbers are bigger and the risks and opportunities greater, but by and large we're all just trying to deliver results through a team of people.'

TIP
Andrew's three tips for being a world-class manager

1. Emotional intelligence

To deliver results through people you need to genuinely care for them and to show empathy. You must understand the people in the team that you're working with – what's important, what makes them tick and how you can alter your style and approach to get the best out of everyone in the team. This is the most important skill for a leader or manager.

2. Influencing skills

It's no good just being able to understand people, however, if you cannot communicate and influence them. If you're spending all your time understanding them without then being able to use that information to influence them to do what is required for the business, then it's a waste of time.

3. Boldness

If you are stepping up from line manager to leader then you need to be prepared to make decisions and set challenges that may sometimes make people feel uncomfortable. If you have the above two skills, which is to understand if it is going to make people feel uncomfortable but then have the ability to communicate the challenge in a way that helps them to see how they can get there so that it isn't just a pipe dream, then you can get their buy-in.

But remember, none of this is useful without excellence in execution in the core role. This is core to being a world-class manager.

04
Inspiring appraisals: How to have quality conversations

Introduction

Everyone hates appraisals. A study of 1,056 organizations in 53 countries by HR consultancy Mercer in 2016 found 95 per cent of managers were dissatisfied with their organization's performance management system.[1] Meanwhile research with more than 1,000 organizations by Bersin™, Deloitte Consulting LLP, showed that performance management had a -60 Net Promoter Score.[2]

Appraisals are costly. Gallup research suggests the cost of lost time spent on performance evaluation ranges from $2.4 million to $35 million a year for a firm with 10,000 employees.[3]

Appraisals are ineffective at predicting performance. Wharton School's George W Taylor professor of management Peter Cappelli says only 27 per cent of next year's appraisal scores can be predicted or explained by this year's scores. According to Cappelli, appraisals are also disengaging as, by default, most of us will be average but 80 per cent of us believe we are better than that, so are not best pleased to get a '3'.[4] And appraisals are biased: the most likely predictor of a higher score is if the appraiser and appraisee are similar.

So why, when traditional performance reviews are so bad they make performance worse about one-third of the time and 77 per cent of HR directors say performance evaluations are not an accurate indication of employee performance, does the appraisal still feature so strongly in a manager's role?

To answer this question, let's first stand back and look at what exactly an appraisal is. A performance appraisal is a review of an employee's job performance and overall contribution to a company. This review, which has traditionally been once a year, is used to highlight the strengths and the weaknesses of the employee in order to improve future performance to deliver better outcomes for the organization.

Done well, an appraisal can not only benefit the business but also the individual, helping them grow professionally. However, the difficulty for managers comes when appraisals are linked to promotion and pay. And, according to Mercer's 2019 Global Performance Management study, 85 per cent of companies link performance and pay.[5]

Appraisals can therefore be one of the trickiest undertakings for managers, especially if you have just stepped into the role and gone from being a 'mate' to a 'manager'.

I get this. I remember having to go into an appraisal conversation with one particular colleague in which I had to rate him on a scale of one to five. I knew that if I gave this colleague a four or five he would get a pay increase. And a pay rise was going to be important to him as he and his partner were trying to get a mortgage to buy a house. So if I could argue my case well enough to my boss as to why he was a four on purely subjective evidence, then he will get that four, and that pay rise. And I like the guy. We're friends. But in reality I knew this colleague was a three. So it was a difficult situation to handle.

Given this, it's no wonder that a number of companies have removed forced rankings and the standardized and infrequent 'appraisal process' – a system Cappelli calls the Santa Performance

Appraisal (Have you been good this year? What would you like then?). In this 'big appraisal shift', companies such as Adobe and IBM have moved towards a more informal way of having quality conversations that happen more often.

World-class managers have these important conversations on a regular basis. And the best conversations are what I call Inspiring Appraisal conversations, at least for the person who's being 'appraised'. This is key, as we're trying to get the best out of people, and we're often at our best when we're focusing on our strengths and talents.

Think back to your experience with a manager or someone more senior to you that you've worked with. How have they impacted how you feel – about yourself, your team and the organization you work for? Your relationship with the people in your team has the biggest impact on how they see themselves, their team and their company.

There is something that all of us can do to impact this in a positive way, pretty quickly. It's about the quality of the conversation we have with our team members. Inspiring Appraisals use inspiring conversations, and the best inspiring conversations are appreciative conversations.

What is an appreciative conversation?

An appreciative conversation is one in which you and the person you are speaking to reach a shared understanding. It is a positive conversation intended to strengthen connections through the use of appreciative language. As a manager you can ask questions which give space for reflection rather than requiring an immediate correct answer. Liz Sebag-Montefiore, co-founder and director at career management company 10Eighty, puts it well when she describes an appreciative conversation as one that:

> centres on creating opportunities for active listening and
> collaborative discussion that helps identify best practice and

improved knowledge of what will drive the achievement of desired outcomes. [Managers should] aim to identify opportunities to make changes that will facilitate continued learning, growth and improvement. It's important to emphasize that this is a collaborative conversation about working together to achieve the outcomes that matter to 'us', rather than a directive-fuelled imposition of changes to be made and goals to be met.

Appreciative conversations have a positive psychological effect on us and they are good for our own performance. It doesn't mean you shouldn't address any of the negative issues, but you do that from a different place that seeks to build someone and which is inspirational. Such conversations are employee-centred, and being employee-centred is what world-class managers do.

When it comes to appraisals you are in the hot seat. Research from Kluger and DeNisi found that at least 30 per cent of performance reviews fail as they end up in decreased employee performance, so approaching appraisals the right way is critical if you are to have the desired positive outcome of improved performance.[6]

As a manager, you need to balance the potentially conflicting needs of a number of different parties. All of the below entities require something from the person you are appraising:

- The organization
- The other people in their team
- The departments that interface with that individual
- The customer
- The individual themselves
- You as the manager

Understanding the individual, their hopes and dreams, their background, their challenges and their ambitions is key to being able to help them to get the best from themselves. Remember that, as with anything to do with people, there is no one-size-fits-all approach. Some of your people will want frequent validation, reassurance, praise or recognition. They need frequent check-ins and for their presence and contribution to be noticed.

Others happily work under their own steam, under the radar, self-directed and autonomous for months on end. As a manager, you will want stronger teams made up of individuals who are able to take greater ownership and act with more autonomy. This will give you more time to concentrate on building key stakeholder relationships, which are both good for your team and also for your own progression. To be a world-class appraiser you should work out which team members fit into which type and approach your appraisals accordingly.

Here's how you do this.

The WCM 7

- Prepare, prepare, prepare!
- Ensure there are no surprises.
- Accentuate the positive.
- Mind your tone – make sure it is constructive.
- Set the right expectation.
- Listen actively and ask good questions.
- Follow up on any commitments.

1. Prepare, prepare, prepare!

Great preparation is absolutely central to having a great appraisal conversation. In fact, if you don't prepare well, you are missing a great opportunity. Appraisal conversations are fantastic opportunities to send a powerful, motivational message to your team member that shows them you truly care about them and their development.

One-to-one meetings are designed so you can concentrate on each member of your team individually and regularly. Your team may feel intimidated or scared about having a one-to-one with you, but you need to put their mind at rest and let them know it is for them to share feedback, good or bad. Yet research from Kluger and DeNisi (1996) found that one in five employees believes their manager doesn't even think about the appraisal until they are in the room with them. So, what can you do to make the appraisals you give work for you, your team member and the organization?

Explain why you are having the appraisal

Clarify expectations
Make it clear that this is a meeting for your appraisee to talk about what's on their mind, share any feedback, offer them mentoring or coaching and discuss their personal development. This will remove any negative thoughts about the meeting.

Don't talk about projects
Talking about specific projects can be a waste of your one-to-one time. Appraisal one-to-ones should focus on the team member, discussing subjects like any mentoring or coaching needs, personal development and personal or team issues.

Decide on the format

Meeting length
If you want to get the full value out of one-to-one meetings, you need time to dig into topics. I suggest leaving an hour for a more detailed appraisal to show it is not just a catch-up. You can always end early, which is much easier than trying to rush a discussion when you have another meeting on the calendar to head to.

Location
Find somewhere that is private so that your appraisee feels it is a safe space to discuss confidential issues. It doesn't always have

to be in a formal meeting room; you could do them in the café or going for a walk. Just think about what would make your appraisee comfortable.

Occurrence
It is vital to hold your one-to-ones regularly rather than waiting for a year to bring everything up. Your people will appreciate more regular feedback and you can quickly discuss and tackle any ideas or problems since your last meeting. You will soon get to know how often your people want or need to have their one-to-one meetings with you, so always try to keep to that schedule. If you do have to cancel a one-to-one meeting make sure you rearrange it immediately, so team members know that you value them.

Choose the frequency
Demands on the team mean it is not always easy to organize weekly meetings but try to make your one-to-one meetings part of your working week.

Scheduling
Many of us are overwhelmed with our existing workload so fitting in one-to-ones with team members can be hard. However, we recommend that as a minimum you should have a one-to-one with your team at least every six weeks.

How many in a team
The more people you personally manage the harder it is to fit everyone in (and do the day job), but setting aside at the very least 30 minutes per person every six weeks is essential to ensure you are keeping on top of any team issues or relevant information.

New starters
A new starter is going to need far more knowledge and guidance than someone more established in the team, so making time for them at the start is essential to ensure they settle into their role – ideally one a week or fortnight until they feel comfortable.

So do take time to prepare well and get your team member to do the same. Here are some great preparation questions to consider:

REVIEW
Preparation questions

- What's your goal for the appraisal?
- How can you make it feel as positive and constructive as possible?
- What positives can you highlight? And what can you praise – it is called an appraisal after all.
- Is there any challenging feedback you need to deliver? And how can you best do that? Do you have evidence to back it up?
- What will the appraisee want to discuss? And what feedback may they have for you?
- How can you get the appraisee to bring their thoughts and ideas to the meeting – about how they are performing, next steps and what support they may need from you?

All this preparation will ensure that you and your team member can have a motivational and meaningful conversation on the day.

2. Ensure there are no surprises

An appraisal should not be the place where new surprising feedback is given, particularly if it is challenging feedback. This could derail the conversation completely.

If your appraisal catches your team member off guard, then you have not been managing that employee well enough during the year. World-class managers have ongoing performance conversations, with feedback being given in a timely fashion throughout the year. It's a bit like a coach coaching as the game is happening, rather than waiting till the end of the game.

There are three main styles of coaching: indirect, directive and situational. The individual being coached and the situation should determine which style you choose.

Indirect coaching

The idea behind this is to get the individual to solve the problem themselves rather than you telling them what to do. It involves taking the time to help the person being coached to arrive at the problem and solution through asking pertinent questions, listening, withholding any judgement and – importantly – holding back any impulse to 'tell' and solve the issue quickly.

Directive coaching

This primarily involves telling. A manager with superior knowledge imparts that knowledge to the individual by telling them what to do. The plus is that the individual learns from the manager. The minus is that it means things will always be done in the same way so there is little room for innovation and change. In some circumstances, however, this is the right approach to take. For example, if the individual is very inexperienced or there is no need to change process. But ensure this does not turn into micromanagement.

Situational coaching

This aims to achieve the perfect balance between indirect and directive coaching. Its application should be determined by the individual and coachee. Some people need more direction and others don't. As a manager, you will need to understand your team members fully to determine what balance to take.

3. Accentuate the positive

Want to know why you need to accentuate the positive? Well, according to the Society of Human Resource Management, 30 per cent of workers are so discouraged by negative feedback that they actively seek new employment. Imagine if close to a third of your team came out of an appraisal you had given and immediately started looking for a new job. It wouldn't bode well for you, the rest of your team or your organization.

It's important to understand that humans are hardwired to react more strongly to negative events such as criticism or negative feedback. It's how our brain has developed from the early days of human history when we needed to be aware of dangerous or negative threats in order to survive. In fact, psychologists have come up with a term for this – negativity bias. We tend to pay more attention to negative information, even if much of the information we have been given is positive. Think about how you had a great day but then one bad thing happened. I bet you spend more time fixating on that one bad thing than remembering all those good things.

Now consider this in the context of an appraisal. You have sat down with your team member and noted all their strengths and what has gone well. Then you move to areas in which that team member needs some development. If you aren't careful about how you phrase this (see point 4 below), then that person will likely come out of the appraisal dwelling on those comments about how they can improve and getting upset about them, rather than feeling happy about all the positive comments.

So, before you conduct the appraisal, ask yourself: what is your positive intention for it? Research suggests that a healthy ratio for positive to developmental feedback is at least 3:1.[7] What ratio do you normally achieve? If it is skewed one way or the other, then spend some time outlining how you can get a better balance.

4. Mind your tone – make sure it is constructive

Tone is critical – it affects how your message is received. As noted in point 3, people can become defensive or angry when facing what they see as criticism.

A manager's tone in feedback scenarios is critical in how it leaves a person feeling. Make sure that you adopt a positive, constructive tone, even if you are discussing challenging issues.

Don't be rude, uncaring or dismissive in how you deliver negative feedback.

This is particularly important if you are giving feedback to millennials – those born between 1981 to 1996, and Gen Z – those born between 1997 and 2012, who came into the workforce in the early 21st century. As best-selling author Simon Sinek notes, the millennial generation craves feedback. However, in practice, he says, 'what they seem to want is more positive feedback, more affirmation when they do well.' Sinek notes that too many of them are not that good at receiving negative feedback.[8]

There are some techniques for giving negative feedback in addition to making sure your tone is constructive:

- Make sure you are calm and emotionally prepared for the appraisal session.
- Book a private space for the meeting so no one else can hear what is being said.
- Ensure the feedback is based on the behaviour and not the person.
- Keep the feedback specific to the particular issue.
- Be candid and sincere.
- Be direct and clear.
- Encourage self-reflection, allowing the employee to respond and listening to their perspective.

When giving feedback, carrot tends to work better than stick. Positive reinforcement, praise and encouragement are more likely to inspire and engage than blame, nit-picking and overdue feedback. If you want to see positive action, aim to leave the person feeling motivated to act, rather than negatively judged and criticized.

> **TIP**
> WCM Tip
>
> Watch yourself speak. Do this by standing in front of a mirror while reading the same paragraph or record yourself on your phone or an online platform like Zoom or Microsoft Teams. Watch your face carefully, paying special attention to how your mouth moves and to your facial expressions. Which facial expressions don't seem to be helping you appear friendly? Lose them!

5. Set the right expectation

Do you think about the skill and competence level of the appraisee when you are setting expectations? Making sure we get the balance right between challenge and support is important. It is good to stretch people in terms of their development, but make sure that stretch doesn't turn into stress because of unrealistic expectations on your part.

Many high-performing managers have very high expectations of themselves and others – and that can be a good thing. But you need to be mindful about what you are asking others to do. It needs to be realistic and you must make sure you don't judge everyone by your own high standards. Sometimes people have different abilities and motivations and we don't want to set people up to fail.

One way to set the right expectations is to use the Challenge/Support tool (Figure 4.1). This helps you to think about the skill and competence level of the appraisee when you are setting expectations. Take some time to fill in the Challenge/Support chart with some possible tasks that you may want to delegate to colleagues or team members. Test if you are setting the level right.

Making sure you get the balance right between challenge and support is important as it is good to stretch people in terms of their development but you don't want to turn that stretch into stress because of unrealistic expectations on your part.

Figure 4.1   Challenge/Support tool

HIGH SUPPORT

Under Achievement
Low standards
Under achievement
Complacency
Inferior knowledge
Low expectations
Lack of innovation

Empowerment
High expectations
High achievement
High standards
Co-operation
Risk taking
Tolerance of mistakes
Trying new ways
High morale

LOW CHALLENGE

HIGH CHALLENGE

Apathy
Very low standards
Low morale
Very low expectations
Lack of team spirit
No innovative ideas

Anxiety
High expectations
Uneven achievement
Variable standards
Competition
Aversion to risk
Blame culture
Fear of failure
Low morale

LOW SUPPORT

6. Listen actively and ask good questions

A great appraisal should have a healthy talk ratio, where the appraisee is talking more than the appraiser. Do be mindful of this and show your interest and curiosity by asking great questions and giving them space to answer.

I once heard appraisals referred to as a dialogue, not a monologue, and I think that is a great way to think about it. So often people do not feel like they are listened to. By carefully and thoughtfully listening to the appraisee you are already delivering a more positive experience for them. This is especially true when delivering more challenging feedback. It is a chance for the appraisee to put forward their side.

By actively listening you can also learn useful information about how the appraisee views their role, garner ideas from them as to improvements that can be made and gather information about their thoughts on the organization as a whole and you as a manager.

So, think about the typical talk ratio in one of your appraisal or review conversations. Do you listen more than you talk – and have you got the balance right?

The talk ratio

To reduce your talk ratio:

- Ask for your appraisee's feedback before the appraisal. Your appraisee will know that you want to hear their thoughts.

- Ask more questions. By asking questions it will move the conversation to the appraisee.

- Active listening. Instead of focusing on how you want to respond to what the appraisee has said, you need to listen actively and let them finish what they are saying. If you only think about your own response you could zone out, interrupt them or use body language to signify that you want the other person to stop talking.

To increase your talk ratio:

- Have confidence to speak. Sometime appraisals can be repetitive and the format may seem the same. But try to have confidence in what you can input and share great ideas/suggestions on anything that doesn't work or could be improved.

- Use verbal bridges to transition to your points. For example, 'I agree X is important [bridge]… and, building on that, I'd like to discuss Y.'

- Practise. Before you hold your appraisal you should practise what you want to say. We know this might not always be possible, but try to think about the key points you want to get across and test out how to say them.

7. Follow up on any commitments

Finally, you must make sure you follow up on any commitments and get the team member to do the same. Schedule a follow-up meeting to allow time for reflections and to pick up on next steps. This will reinforce your commitment to them and show that you take the process and their development seriously.

Failing to follow up gives out a negative message. Your apprai-see will think they have wasted their time on the appraisal. You could also forget valuable information mentioned in the appraisal. Lack of follow-up makes people think you have just gone through the motions because you have to and that you don't care. So, forget this step at your peril.

Conclusion

As noted at the start of this chapter, appraisals are often loathed by managers and their team members. But if you conduct appraisals like a world-class manager does, employing the tactics outlined above, they will be one of the most useful tools to develop your team, motivate them and drive productivity. If we aim to leave people feeling that we care about them and their development and that we will provide all the support they need, we can help them develop and reach their potential. This is then a win for you, for your team member and for the organization.

Of course, getting the best out of appraisals means you need to devote some time to them – in preparation, delivery and follow-up. And we all know managers never have enough time. So, let's jump into the next chapter and discover how world-class managers best optimize their time.

Chapter review

Questions for reflection

As you consider your role as a world-class manager, reflect on the following questions and capture them in a way that works for you. Write notes, start a journal, record on your phone or capture on a spreadsheet – whichever will enable you to remember these points when dealing with your team and other people in your organization:

- How well do you support your team?
- How do you communicate?
- How well do you inspire your team?
- Take a moment to think about the things that make you feel great at work. What are they?
- Now think about your team… what would make them feel really great at work?
- What can you do to make that happen?

Actions to take now

- Have a conversation with a number of team members to evaluate the current appraisal 'process'.
- Think about how you can better align the conversations to the team's/department's/organization's goals. Get more information if required.
- Create an evaluation process for yourself. How can you get your people to rate the experience you deliver? Measure this.

Notes

1 Mercer (2016) Compensation Planning and Performance Management. www.mercer.com/content/dam/mercer/attachments/global/webcasts/gl-2016-talent-compensation-planning-performance-management-mercer.pdf (archived at perma.cc/3LCU-UQLY)

2 O'Connell, B (2020) Performance Management Evolves, SHRM. www.shrm.org/hr-today/news/all-things-work/pages/performance-management-evolves.aspx (archived at perma.cc/YEE2-V668)

3 Goodwin, J, Morris, D, Scott, G and Davis, J (2019) Transforming Performance Management Part 1, Deloitte. www2.deloitte.com/us/en/blog/human-capital-blog/2019/transforming-performance-management-part-1.html (archived at perma.cc/737B-UWAG)

4 Sutton, R and Wigert, B (2019) More Harm than Good: The Truth about Performance Reviews, Gallup. www.gallup.com/workplace/249332/harm-good-truth-performance-reviews.aspx (archived at perma.cc/3TFY-E8KP)

5 Harrington, S (2019) Five Things to Consider When Redesigning Performance Management – from Peter Cappelli. www.thepeoplespace.com/ideas/articles/five-things-consider-when-redesigning-performance-management (archived at perma.cc/3X65-ERMA)

6 Mercer (2019) Global Performance Management Study. www.mercer.com/our-thinking/career/voice-on-talent/performance-management-and-coronavirus-outbreak.html?bsrc=mercer (archived at perma.cc/9XLM-4KEW)

7 Kluger, A N and DeNisi, A (1996) The Effects of Feedback Interventions on Performance: A historical review, a meta-analysis, and a preliminary feedback intervention theory. *Psychological Bulletin*, 119(2), 254–84. doi.org/10.1037/0033-2909.119.2.254 (archived at perma.cc/S2WD-5H5K)

8 Hogan, M (2016) 5 Employee Feedback Stats That You Need to See. www.linkedin.com/business/talent/blog/talent-strategy/employee-feedback-stats-you-need-to-see (archived at perma.cc/4RLN-ENN3)

9 Sinek, S (2017) *Leaders Eat Last: Why some teams pull together and others don't*. Penguin Random House, New York

05
Optimizing your time

Introduction

Time. It's the most precious resource we have as human beings and yet there is never enough of it. Today it feels that we're busier than ever, emailing more than ever, meeting more than ever, WhatsApping more than ever and, for most organizations, being reviewed by customers more than ever.

How many times have you heard the phrase 'you can't get anything done around here' in your workplace? It may seem like people are just being grumpy but there is much evidence behind this sentiment. Let's look at just a few statistics.

The average company loses more than 20 per cent of its productive power to what Bain & Company's Michael Mankins and Eric Garton call organizational drag – all the processes, practices and structures that waste time and limit output. They say that, in their work with clients, they generally find that 25 per cent or more of the typical line manager's time is wasted in unnecessary meetings or e-communications.[1] In other words, as a manager you are probably spending more than a day a week doing nothing but interactions that do not benefit your team or organization – answering emails you didn't need to be copied into or in meetings that do not ultimately enable a business outcome or add value to customers.

Research from Leslie A Perlow and Eunice Eun from Harvard Business School and Constance Noonan Hadley from Boston University Questrom School of Business across diverse industries found only 17 per cent of executives reported their meetings were generally productive uses of group and individual time. A separate survey of 182 senior managers by the same team found two-thirds of managers (65 per cent) felt meetings kept them from completing their own work, 71 per cent said meetings were inefficient and unproductive, 64 per cent that they prevented deep thinking and 62 per cent that they missed opportunities to bring the team closer together.[2]

Meanwhile a study of 20 organizations by Simone Kauffeld of Technische Universität Braunschweig, and Nale Lehmann-Willenbrock of the University of Amsterdam, found that 'dysfunctional meeting behaviours', such as criticizing, wandering off the topic and complaining, were associated with lower levels of employment stability, innovation and market share.[3]

Sarah (not her real name), an executive at a media company with whom I have collaborated in the past, knows all about this. Every month she had to produce a detailed report on the performance of her product lines for that month. Sarah was in charge of 11 products and the report covered revenue and profit/losses for each product together with an explanation as to why these were achieved or not, planned initiatives and predicted revenues going forward, potential bottlenecks and concerns and what was being done about them, plus any people issues. She also had to include reports from the line managers within her unit. The overall report averaged 15 A4 pages and took up a full day each month to compile.

Every executive in the business produced a similar report and they were compiled and sent out to all the members of the senior team in advance of a monthly meeting where the performance of the business was discussed. Sarah was expected to read this final report before attending the meeting.

So, you would expect the subsequent meeting to pick out the most salient points and drill down into challenging areas, coming up with interventions to tackle them, wouldn't you?

Wrong, says Sarah. Instead, every month an entire morning was taken out of her busy schedule for a meeting in which each participant ran through the exact same information already contained in their report. 'I sat for four or five hours listening to a repeat of everything I had read the night before. It was such a waste of time and very little positive action came out of it,' she told me. 'We could have achieved more in a focused, outcomes-based meeting of no more than one hour. I came to hate those meetings, which were not only unproductive and draining but also, I felt, sent out a negative message about the culture of the business.'

Just think about this. Each one of these performance review meetings took four hours a month. Requesting, chasing and collating reports from team members took two hours. Working through the financial data provided in advance, checking answers to questions and writing her report took another five to six hours. Reading the final business unit report another one. That is 12 hours a month on this one report. Multiply that by 12 months and then by every person in the business who had to do the same activity and you are talking about thousands of hours lost in that one company alone.

Every message, every meeting and every request places a demand on our time – and this is not just affecting our ability to do our jobs better but is having an impact on our emotional and mental wellbeing. Happiness researcher and author Ashley Whillans analysed a survey of 2.5 million Americans by the Gallup Organization and found that 8 in 10 respondents did not have the time they wanted each day. Whillans talks about a 'time famine' – a collective failure to manage time. This time poverty exists across all economic strata and across many continents. It's so bad that Whillans and her team's analysis found time stress had a stronger negative effect on happiness than being unemployed.[4]

Meetings are without a doubt a source of upset in organizations, as we have already seen. And the COVID-19 pandemic has had an impact on these. As many people moved to working from home during lockdowns across the world, particularly knowledge workers, the number of meetings increased. According to aggregated meeting and email meta-data of 3,143,270 users released by the

National Bureau of Economic Research, there was a 12.9 per cent increase in the number of meetings per person and a 13.5 per cent rise in the number of attendees per meeting compared to pre-pandemic levels. There were also significant increases in the length of the average workday, up 8.2 per cent or 48.5 minutes longer than pre-pandemic.

However, the average length of these meetings decreased by 20.1 per cent, so in reality we spent 11.5 per cent less time in meetings during this time.[5] Anecdotal evidence suggests the increase in meetings may have resulted from the need for managers to check in more frequently and have social conversations with team members working from home. It remains to be seen whether this trend will continue as organizations move back to office-based work, at least for some of the time.

But it's not just about meetings. Research from Microsoft Workplace discovered a huge increase in instant messages sent during work-from-home periods. There was a 72 per cent rise overall and a dramatic 115 per cent increase in instant messages sent by managers during March 2020.[6]

We know that our attention spans are shrinking, the working week is getting longer, competition is more ferocious and we're retiring later and later. You've probably lost attention already! So, optimizing and managing time is one of the biggest weapons in the armoury of the world-class manager.

Our work with managers across the world has discovered that taking some time out to stop and think about what's going on in the team is a trait of the world-class manager. And it doesn't have to be much time. Just one hour a month makes a difference. Using this hour to look at key processes, interactions and stakeholders, all with the view of 'how can we, as a team, be more efficient?', is a smart way to spend a little time.

As a manager you do have a choice over how you choose to view time. Successful sports people, for example, often describe moments when time seems to slow down when they are living in the moment, giving them an ability to think and act like truly world-class athletes. We may not all be athletes, but the principle is exactly the same. Slowing our own thoughts down has the same effect on how we manage ourselves and our team's time day to day.

So how can you optimize your time? Here are the seven actions we have seen performed by world-class managers.

The WCM 7

- Take control of your time.
- Use the Urgent–Important Matrix.
- Prioritize tasks for achievement.
- Learn to say no.
- Reset the dial.
- Follow the 80/20 rule.
- Take a 2-minute Power Prep.

1. Take control of your time

Great time managers are very protective of their time. They make sure they focus on 'the right stuff' and are ruthless at weeding out any unnecessary activity or distraction.

This is easier said than done. We may say we don't have enough time, but how many of us equate being busy with our popularity and importance? In fact, academics Silvia Bellessa, Neetu Pahari a and Anat Keinan looked at just this in research on how 'busyness' (long hours of remunerated employment and lack of leisure time) impacts perceptions of status. They find that feeling busy and over-worked may make us feel in demand and scarce, and therefore more valuable and important.

'The positive status effect of displaying one's busyness and lack of leisure time is driven by the perception that a busy person possesses desired human capital characteristics (competence, ambition) and is scarce and in demand in the job market,' they say.[7]

Table 5.1   Time activity table

Time	Activity
09.00–10.00	Checked and replied to emails 9.00–9.30 Weekly team meeting 9.30–10.00
10.00–11.00	Customer call 10.05–10.12 Dial-in with Sophie 10.15–10.30 Prep for meeting with manager 10.30–10.50 Sam asked for chat 10.50
11.00–12.00	Coffee 11.00–11.10 Checked emails again 11.10–11-20 Reviewed report from manager 11.20–12.00

As we've seen, creating space to think is a trait of world-class managers. So, ditch the mindset that being busy is a sign of management competence and think about how you use your time. How often do you review how you spend your time?

Here are some tips to start taking control of your time.

Undertake a time audit

First, map out how you are currently using your time. You can start by taking one day and breaking it down into hours or major activities using a time activity table like that shown in Table 5.1. Then try this for the full working week. At the end of the week, analyse where you are spending time and if there are ways in which you can take more control of that time.

Plan the night before

Planning your day the night before sets you up so you are focused on how you spend time during that day. It helps keep you in check with what is required of you.

Schedule your time

Try to block out your time in chunks. If possible, only book meetings, webinars or calls when your time is less in demand; for example, if after lunch time is slightly less busy for you, then schedule them here. Also, only allow others to book up your time in your diary in these times too.

2. Use the Urgent–Important Matrix

The Urgent–Important Matrix is a classic model of time management. It is used by many managers the world over to help them prioritize and better manage their time.

Let's take a look at how it works.

Figure 5.1   Urgent–Important Matrix 1

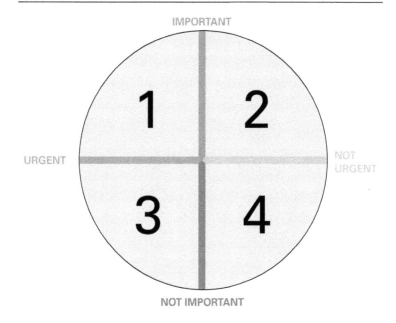

Box 1: Urgent and important activity

This is deadline-driven and non-negotiable. It could be a last-minute deadline from your boss, signing an important contract or covering for a colleague who is ill. There may be negative consequences for not doing it now, for example losing an important customer or enabling a crisis to get worse.

- **Time Tip:** Be mindful of 'fire-fighting' and last-minute types of activity falling into this box. Look at the activities you have put in Box 1 and consider whether you could have planned better or whether they are now in this box because you procrastinated and put them off.

Box 2: Not urgent but important activity

This is activity that is critical for leadership but not immediately urgent. It includes areas such as strategic thinking, planning ahead on projects and trying to apply foresight and vision; crucial review activity like improving service or processes; working on relationships with customers and stakeholders; and having quality one-to-ones with your team.

- **Time Tip:** This is a box that managers should be spending much more time in. It's very high-value activity and it is an area that can often get squeezed if we are not managing our time well. Ensure you schedule regular time for this work. Could you plan better and free up time to spend more time in Box 2?

Box 3: Urgent but not important activity

This work is not necessarily important but it is urgent and it can take up a lot of your time. Often these are people-related activities such as a workplace question from a colleague. That person may think it is urgent but it doesn't actively contribute to your long-term goals. Emails often fall into this box.

- **Time Tip:** Can you remove some of the activity from this box either by delegation or by simply saying 'no', respectfully, of course? Do those messages you have received really require an immediate response? One approach is to create allocated times in the day to deal with emails and calls.

Box 4: Not urgent and not important activity

This activity is basically a distraction. Scrolling through social media is a perfect example. You may have looked at LinkedIn to check out a particular person and before you know it you have spent 20 minutes reading posts.

- **Time Tip:** Weed this out! You may be able to automate some of this work or, better still, delete it altogether.

In Figure 5.2 you can see what this may look like in practice.

Figure 5.2   Urgent–Important Matrix 2 filled in

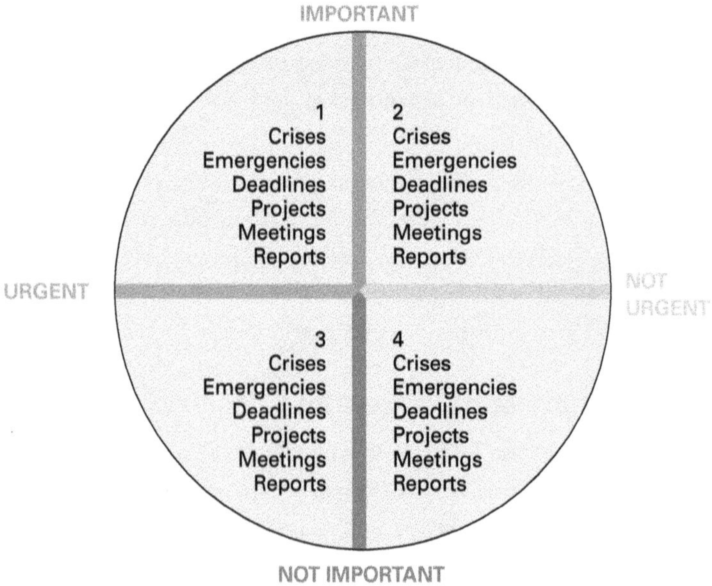

IMPORTANT

1	2
Crises	Crises
Emergencies	Emergencies
Deadlines	Deadlines
Projects	Projects
Meetings	Meetings
Reports	Reports

URGENT

NOT URGENT

3	4
Crises	Crises
Emergencies	Emergencies
Deadlines	Deadlines
Projects	Projects
Meetings	Meetings
Reports	Reports

NOT IMPORTANT

The Urgent–Important Matrix helps world-class managers to be rigorous about the way they manage their time so they can spend time on the high-value activities that particularly sit in Box 2.

3. Prioritize tasks for achievement

Isn't it great when you feel you have achieved something? It may be that you have finally completed a 10k run having barely got off the sofa just six months earlier. Or you have finished writing the first chapter of that book you have been planning for many years. Or perhaps you have just ticked off your to-do list for that day. Whenever you achieve something you get a real sense of satisfaction.

That feeling is backed up by research. One study, for example, found that achievement goals are positively related to life satisfaction.

So, start each day by taking 10 minutes to plan and prioritize your tasks. Define the top two to three and look at how achievable they are. Achieving a task releases energy to tackle the bigger stuff.

Do you know when you have the most energy? By managing your energy as well as your time you will be more effective. Energy levels are different from person to person. Do the most difficult tasks when your energy is high and the more mundane and less important ones when your energy levels are low. So, if you're a morning person who is at the top of their game at the first crack of dawn, you should schedule the more difficult, mind-boggling tasks at that time. If you are a night owl, then prioritize the other way round.

When prioritizing tasks, think about the these actions:

Do: complete the task now.

Defer: complete it later.

Delegate: assign it to someone else.

Delete: remove it from your list.

4. Learn to say no

How often have you seen a job description asking for someone with a 'can-do' attitude? Organizations love someone who is positive and willing to take on a challenge. But beware. This can be a double-edged sword. If you have too much on, you may need to say no sometimes.

We often commit to too much, thinking we have more time than we do. This is known as the planning fallacy and research backs up the idea that we anticipate that we will finish our tasks earlier than we do.[8] We are too optimistic and therefore prone to say yes to more things than we have time to accomplish.

But saying no is hard. Many of us are hardwired to want to please people, especially if it is your boss or a team member. We worry the recipient of our 'no' may view that denial as rejection. As a manager, we feel that saying no may look like we can't handle our workload. It can take some practice to say no!

How to say no

- Explain why you are saying no. Don't just say you don't have enough time – people who make time-related excuses are perceived as less trustworthy and likeable than those who do not.[9] We all have the same 24 hours a day, so it is seen as a personal preference not to say yes. Instead, explain you are saying no because of something out of your control, such as a project deadline, customer commitment or the fact it doesn't fit with the organization's strategic goals.

- Consider whether the activity you are being asked about would fit better with someone else's expertise. For example, if you are asked to organize a project that isn't in your job description, suggest someone on your team or in your network for whom the request would be appropriate.

- Be polite when you say no. Thank them for thinking of you or suggesting the initiative but say you are unable to take it on now. If it isn't urgent but is something you would like to do and adds value to your team or business, then suggest when you may be able to get onto it.

- Don't put your hand up when your organization asks for volunteers for work you haven't time to take on!

5. Reset the dial

So many managers I meet are incredibly stretched by the sheer volume of their workloads. They sometimes literally have no space to pause and gather their thoughts as they rush from task to task. This can really impact on their effectiveness and also on their sense of wellbeing.

Amy Jen Su talks about 'white space' – time you unexpectedly find you have.[10] It may be that a meeting is cancelled or rescheduled or a train journey takes longer than usual. So often we waste this time, scrolling through our phone messages or social media for example. Instead, why not use this to reset the dial, to decompress and give yourself that space to refocus?

Managing your energy is a key focus for every modern manager. Even taking a few minutes to pause, to refocus – and to close your eyes and concentrate on your breathing – can make all the difference to your effectiveness.

6. Follow the 80:20 rule

In 1906 Italian economist Vilfredo Pareto observed that about 80 per cent of Italy's land was owned by 20 per cent of the population. When carrying out surveys in a number of other countries he found that a similar distribution applied. Thus was founded the Pareto principle, otherwise known as the 80:20 rule.

When applied to business, the rule can be understood as 80 per cent of your outcomes come from 20 per cent of your inputs. For example, 80 per cent of results come from 20 per cent of employees. Or 80 per cent of your sales come from just 20 per cent of your customers.

When world-class managers think about where they spend their time, they keep this principle in mind. What is the best 20 per cent of activity you can focus on that will give you 80 per cent of value? Can you prioritize your workload accordingly?

Given that only 52 per cent of 1,500 executives surveyed by consultancy McKinsey said the way they spent their time largely matched their organizations' strategic priorities, you will shine if you demonstrate you are spending your time adding value and prioritizing strategically by following this 80:20 rule.[11]

How to 80:20 at work

- Make a list of the 10 things that you spend most of your time on.

- Highlight the two things that truly benefit you and drive your performance. Do these more often.

- Review the rest and remove anything unnecessary. Remember to delegate items wherever possible.

7. Take a 2-minute Power Prep

'By failing to prepare you are preparing to fail'

'Give me six hours to chop down a tree and I will spend the first four sharpening the axe'

'He who is best prepared can best serve his moment of inspiration'

There's a reason there are so many sayings related to preparation. Preparation helps you to focus. It helps reduce your stress. It helps you think about potential problems and anticipate questions. It makes you feel comfortable. And it leads to a more successful outcome.

And yet I bet you regularly find yourself rushing from one meeting to the next without time to properly prepare. Or that you rarely have time to reflect on what was just discussed in the meeting you've just rushed from.

When you are time poor it is easy to skip the preparation. World-class managers know that even two minutes spent preparing will make a difference to their impact. I call this the 2-minute

Power Prep. Being clear on the answers to the following questions will help you make the most effective use of your time in that activity.

The 2-minute Power Prep

- What's your objective for the meeting/call/presentation?
- What's the purpose of the meeting/call/presentation?
- Who will be in attendance?
- How do you want to show up and contribute?

Conclusion

Managing your time is one of the trickiest skills for a manager, particularly in the 'always on' world we live in today. It can feel that you are living in a permanent state of overload as more and more tasks fill up your in-tray. Our work with managers has found time management to be one of the biggest, if not the biggest, challenges today. If you master this one skill, then you are well on the way to becoming a world-class manager.

CHECKLIST
Actions to take now

- Review your calendar and ask yourself how you can create more time to focus on the 'important stuff' and be more of a strategic leader.
- Have a personal daily 'plan and review' session at the start of the day, where you plan and prioritize for the day ahead.
- At the end of the day, review your progress. Ask yourself what you and your team would do if you had more time.

Notes

1 Mankins, M and Garton, E (2017) *Time, Talent, Energy: Overcome organizational drag & unleash your team's productive power.* Harvard Business Review Press, Brighton, MA

2 Perlow, L A, Noonan Hadley, C and Eun, E (2017) Stop the Meeting Madness. hbr.org/2017/07/stop-the-meeting-madness (archived at perma.cc/SEX6-R4ZH)

3 Kauffeld, S and Lehmann-Willenbrock, N (2012) Meetings Matter: Effects of team meetings on team and organizational success. *Small Group Research*, 43, 130–58. DOI: 10.1177/1046496411429599.]

4 Whillans, A V (2019) Time for Happiness. hbr.org/2019/01/time-for-happiness (archived at perma.cc/MF7V-RTDD)

5 DeFilippo, E, Michael Imping, S, Single, M, Pilzer, J T and Sadden, R. (2020) Collaborating During Coronavirus: The Impact of COVID-19 on the Nature of Work, National Bureau of Economic Research. www.nber.org/papers/w27612 (archived at perma.cc/T65A-875A)

6 Layne, H and Cossi, G (2020) The Rise of 30-Minute Meetings and Other Ways Collaboration is Changing. workplaceinsights.microsoft.com/workplace-analytics/the-rise-of-shorter-meetings-and-other-ways-collaboration-is-changing-with-remote-work/ (archived at perma.cc/X6N2-694G)

7 Bellezza, S, Pahari, N and Keinon, A (2017) Conspicuous consumption of time: When busyness and lack of leisure time become a status symbol. *Journal of Consumer Research*, 44(**1**, June): 118–38

8 Buehler, R, Griffin, D and Ross, M (1994) Exploring the 'Planning Fallacy': Why people underestimate their task completion times. web.mit.edu/curhan/www/docs/Articles/biases/67_J_Personality_and_Social_Psychology_366,_1994.pdf (archived at perma.cc/6AGQ-76ES)

9 Su, A J (2019) *The Leader You Want To Be: Five essential principles for bringing out your best self every day.* Harvard Business Review Press, Brighton, MA

10   Bregman, P (2013) A Personal Approach to Organizational Time
Management. www.mckinsey.com/business-functions/people-and-
organizational-performance/our-insights/a-personal-approach-to-
organizational-time-management?stcr=1F8DFE5385EE44E6A8BB21
83A2BC8898&cid=other-eml-alt-mip-mck&hlkid=41e01b9ab0314
22997e003113dc600ef&hctky=10404040&hdpid=0a24ac81-ca55-
46fe-88e9-7254df642f73 (archived at perma.cc/2AJN-C7ZN)

06

Improving communications

Introduction

David is people and organizational development director at Dole plc, the global leader in fresh produce operating in 75 countries and which was formed from the merger of Dole Food Company and Total Produce in 2021. Previously in the same role at Total Produce, David says that, as a result of its decentralized organizational model, traditionally there had been very little communication at group level. People felt affiliation to their local business and communication was delivered at that level. Then the COVID-19 pandemic hit – and everything changed. The company needed to reassure its people, explain and emphasize the importance of safety measures – especially as it traded in an essential product, food, with people needing to work together on-site – and to keep motivation up. So it began to communicate more regularly from the centre, in particular through cascading messaging from the chief executive.

One day, says David, a supportive message from the CEO was distributed and the manager of one site sent an email back thanking him for the sentiments. Five minutes later the CEO had picked up the phone and called that manager. They had never talked before. In fact, as far as the manager was concerned the CEO didn't know he existed. This particular site was used as a benchmark for safety practices and the CEO told the manager how impressed he was with what they were doing. They chatted for half an hour. As soon as the call finished the manager came out of his office and told a colleague that the CEO knew about what they were doing there and how it had made his month hearing that.

'I love this simple example which shows the power of communication and community,' says David. 'That reinforcement means that this communication will stick. That guy's going to be telling all his mates and it will spread around the business and all the employees will now know what we're doing here. These little acts become legend. It's the tiniest of things but has a big impact.'

This small action demonstrates the power of communication when handled correctly. As presidential speechwriter and author James Humes eloquently put it: 'The art of communication is the language of leadership.' In other words, mastering communication is an essential skill to being a good manager. Communication is not just about giving out information. There is an 'art' to it and world-class managers are proficient in this art.

Unfortunately, our research found that many managers are not confident when it comes to their communication skills. A third (32.8 per cent) of managers globally are not clear on how and what channels to use and when it is best to communicate with their team. And while nearly 88 per cent of managers feel they always share important information with their team, just one in six (15.7 per cent) regularly seek feedback on their communication style and impact with their team.

So it comes as no surprise then that in our visits to thousands of teams in more than 700 companies and organizations in 50 countries, the one thing nearly all of these companies and all of these teams have in common is that they want communication to be improved.

Communication skills are one of the most in-demand areas when it comes to managers. In a survey of 196 leaders from more than 30 global organizations on the top 10 competencies required by leaders, 'clearly communicates expectations' comes in third place with 56 per cent of respondents saying this is a vital competency and 'communicates openly and often' is in sixth place at 42 per cent.[1]

Futurist and author Bernard Marr cites communication skills as one of seven skills that are vital to success in any field, while McKinsey research identifying foundational skills required to thrive in the future of work names communication as one of the critical cognitive skills groups.[2,3] It breaks this communication group into four key skills: storytelling and public speaking, asking the right questions, synthesizing messages and active listening.

So, you can't be a world-class manager unless you are a great communicator. And the need for great communication skills has become even more critical in a world where your team may be remote, hybrid or on-site, where they may work across different geographic locations and time zones, may include a mix of full-time employees, freelancers and project specific team members – and where there are more tools you can communicate through than ever before.

Great communication is a function of two things: sharing the right information in the right way at the right time in the right place and listening at the right time in the right way. When and where you deliver your message is important to consider. Communication can also be subjective. What I think is great communication might be awful to someone else. We've seen organizations spend millions of dollars to land key messages, for it all to fall over once it hits the manager.

World-class managers play a vital role in helping the flow of messages around an organization, a department and a team. There are three reasons why managers need to be great communicators:

1. Good communication improves employee engagement

Most of what people regard as great engagement is in reality great communication. Helping people feel connected, valued, recognized, receive good feedback and know what is going on – this is all about communicating well. Get this right and engagement improves. But get it wrong, such as through sending excessive emails, and you immediately disengage people. Email is one of the most frustrating things for your people, so if you have to use it send short and clear emails. And remember, when you are sending electronic communication you lose the non-verbal clues you get from face-to-face communication. Without these clues, such as frowns, shrugs or silence, it is harder for you to read the room and change approach. Be aware of the fact electronic communications are open to interpretation.

2. Good communication busts silos

Silos are a problem in nearly every organization. As managers we naturally gravitate to our own teams or departments and focus on our own customers and hitting our KPIs. It is easy to become detached or distant from what is going on around us in the wider organization and how we connect to the greater strategy or vision. However, a key to your success as a manager and to the organization as a whole is the collaboration between teams and departments. Strong cross-departmental interactions enable managers to give and receive feedback and learn from other successes as well as drawing on others' experience to help with improvements.

3. Good communication helps you execute the strategy

Let's be honest, in most companies cascades don't work, despite what leaders think. This is where someone shares something at a senior level and expects, sometimes as if by magic, that a 'cascade' happens and people share information. Our experience with teams finds this often does not happen. In some cases it doesn't matter much, but when it comes to a message related to executing your organization's strategy, then it matters a great deal. Managers are the most trusted channel of communications in an organization.

If you are effective with your communication, then you can make sure the right message is delivered to the right people to push that strategic objective forward.

Managers are the two-way bridge that connects the organization up and down and left and right. Some of the overall organizational communication issues may be out of our control but much is within our gift. Here's how you can make yourself a world-class communicator.

The WCM 7

- Carry out a communications audit.
- Discover your team's communication preferences.
- Use the 5 Ps.
- Share context to create alignment.
- Make communication two-way.
- Seek feedback on your approach.
- The sixth P – positive energy and your personal style.

1. Carry out a communications audit

To improve effectiveness in communication you need to know how effective you currently are, so start by carrying out a communications audit. There are five steps to take.

1. Ask people what they think

Maybe bring together a small group comprising team members and other people you collaborate with to discuss how they feel about organizational communication in general and what can be improved. Then ask them how your own communication can be improved in this context. Be prepared to be uncomfortable and don't take their responses as criticism. Make sure it is a safe space where people can respectfully tell you how you can improve. Remember that becoming more effective in your communication benefits everyone. Clarity equals results.

2. Do wider quantitative and qualitative research

If it doesn't already, ask your organization to include specific communication questions in the employee survey. This can include questions like 'what do you want to know more about?' and 'what do you feel that the organization needs to be more transparent about?' Also use any quantitative metrics from your communications channels. For example, click through rates on emails or Microsoft Teams attendees to see what messages have been effective to date.

3. Follow up the findings

Once you have your research findings go back to anyone that participated in the survey to dig deeper and uncover any issues that need addressing. Again you could hold small focus group sessions and encourage open and honest feedback and solutions.

4. Take action

Once you have received the suggested actions, you will need to separate them out into the timescale of what is doable. What can be done immediately with little cost or negative implications? What is a long-term improvement that may need a budget or timings sign-off?

5. Share the findings and actions

Make sure to share your findings with your team or your organization, in particular the employees that contributed to the research. Highlight the key insights and what is going to happen as a result of the audit and by when.

2. Discover your team's communication preferences

There is so much we could focus on when it comes to communication but, for managers, it's all about where you can make the most impact – and one of the areas in which you can make significant impact is the team briefing. But how well do you know your team's communication preferences? Do you know what they want to know, how often they want to know it and through what channels? Getting clear on these points will really help you tailor your communication to their needs – and will lead to much more productive team briefings.

We all have different preferences when it comes to communication – some people like things short, sharp and to the point; others love detail; some like the story and the big picture; others like the facts and figures. There's no right or wrong – the point is that we are all different and when we communicate we need to match our style to that of our audience or we may not get our message across in the way we'd hoped.

The first thing is to destroy any assumptions you have, perhaps based on your team members' ages, backgrounds or roles. You may think you know your team but, according to Chicago Booth research, people who knew each other well understood each other no better than people who'd just met.[4] Worse still, participants frequently overestimated their ability to communicate and this was more pronounced with people they knew well.

Instead, just ask your team members about their preferences. You can use a simple table like Table 6.1. Write a list of each member of your team and speak with them to establish their preferred method of communication, how often and how much detail they want. While you won't be able to satisfy each individual all of the time, this will help you develop an overall plan.

Table 6.1 Team member preferences

Team member	Preferred method	How often	How much detail

3. Use the 5 Ps

The 5 Ps is a useful model to help us focus and improve our communication.

1. Purpose

Get clear first of all on what is the point of the communication. What are you trying to achieve? For example, is it an update or to address an important issue or is it to inform people on changes in the team or organization? If you are clear then your audience will be.

2. People

A team briefing is a great opportunity to say thank you and to make people feel valued and appreciated. But sometimes you have news to share that will make people uncomfortable. For example, changes in the department, team or business that might affect them. Some people are unsettled by any change, so how you communicate is critical. Allow people to ask questions. If you don't have the answers, it's ok to say 'I don't know, I'll get back to you.' And then make sure you do! One of the most common complaints we hear from people is when their managers promise to get back to them with stuff and then they don't. Also remember we are all human, so do use your communication to talk about personal news: birthdays, new people joining, people marrying or who have done charity work or something exceptional outside of work. All of this adds a feelgood factor to your team briefings and improves relationships. It doesn't have to be all about business.

3. Progress

'How are we doing?' Let people know how well they're doing against their goals and deadlines. Everyone loves to hear they're making progress towards their goals. Share any great successes or exciting new developments. We're looking here to include news that creates positive energy in the team and leaves people feeling really upbeat.

4. Policies

This is the official stuff. Are there any updates or changes on policy issues, CSR, HR or other procedures? Do people need to do anything to comply with the policy changes? Let your people know where they can get information from. As managers we want to reduce the stress and uncertainty people can feel when it comes to 'the official stuff'.

5. Points for action

Make it clear what actions are required, who needs to do them and when they need to do them by. Plus check if they need any support to deliver on the action.

4. Share context to create alignment

World-class managers are good at communicating context and meaning. They help their people understand how their individual contribution fits into the big picture and how they personally can impact it. Check you are communicating each of these elements clearly to your team by referring to the illustration in Figure 6.1.

Figure 6.1   Communicating vision

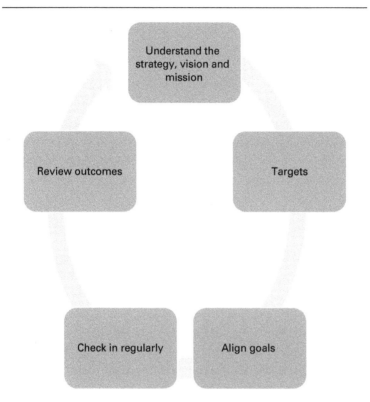

5. Make communication two-way

Two-way communication, where two parties transfer information and listen to each other, is critical to building collaboration and trust within your team. In effect, the communication is negotiated with the objective of ending up with a mutually satisfactory solution.

A good team briefing should not be a one-way tell; there should be as much listening as there is telling and informing. The best way to get your team to speak up is to show them that you appreciate and value their input.

When encouraging your people to speak more, delve deeper into what they are saying to show you are listening and to gain greater clarity of what they mean. Turn negatives into improvement areas. Ask anyone making negative comments to offer suggestions on how to improve.

One hotelier we work with in the UK encourages all managers to hold regular catch-ups with each team member to ask a simple question: 'How are you?' It gives each colleague the opportunity to express how they feel at that moment, whether at work or in their home life. Everyone is encouraged to share how they are feeling to enable issues to be discussed or achievements to be celebrated.

6. Seek feedback

Great managers and communicators are often obsessive about improving their performance in communication. They regularly seek feedback to test if their approach is hitting the mark.

Whenever you ask for feedback, be as specific as possible. If you ask questions like 'how am I doing?' you will likely get a vague answer. If you ask specific questions like 'how did you feel about my presentation, did you feel I covered everything correctly?' you will get a more detailed response.

7. The sixth P – positive energy and your personal style

Your personal style plays an important part in making a team briefing a positive, energizing and worthwhile experience for the team.

Attitude is key. Think about how you can make your team briefings as energizing and as engaging for your team as possible.

- Be more proactive than reactive.
- Smile more.

- Have a sense of humour.
- Think about being positive at the start of your day.
- Try not to moan/complain.
- Avoid speaking negatively about anyone.
- Use positive words.
- Highlight the good things.

Conclusion

Having a high-quality conversation is challenging for many of us. Miscommunication is rife in organizations and it is easy for people to blame others for that rather than to look at themselves. The rise of technology-based means of communication, from the ubiquitous email to text and internal channels like Slack, have muddied the waters further. While enabling more frequent and actionable communication, they are also open to more interpretation than in-person conversations.

Knowing what medium to use for what message is a core skill of world-class managers. For example, one-to-one in-person meetings are best for delivering confidential or sensitive information as these allow information to flow better both ways as well as enabling real-time conversation. Written communication, such as email or instant messaging platforms, is easy and quick, works as a way of documenting thoughts or actions and is useful if you need to impart information to many people.

It's essential to work on your communication skills if you are to become a world-class manager. And it's not just about employees. As we will see in the next chapter, communicating well with the customer is also a key skill.

CHECKLIST
Actions to take now

- Review your team briefing approach through a communications audit and the 5 Ps model.
- Get feedback on your style in terms of content and delivery.
- Think about how you can change your communications to make your team briefings more effective.

Notes

1 Giles, S (2016) The Most Important Leadership Competencies, According to Leaders Around the World. hbr.org/2016/03/the-most-important-leadership-competencies-according-to-leaders-around-the-world (archived at perma.cc/TRS7-45CH)

2 World Economic Forum (2021) 7 Key Soft Skills of Successful People. www.weforum.org/agenda/2021/01/7-key-soft-skills-of-successful-people/ (archived at perma.cc/RN42-P6PD)

3 World Economic Forum (2021) Defining the Skills Citizens Will Need in the Future. www.weforum.org/agenda/2021/06/defining-the-skills-citizens-will-need-in-the-future-world-of-work (archived at perma.cc/W78J-V73X)

4 World Economic Forum (2020) 8 Secrets of Great Communicators. www.weforum.org/agenda/2020/09/8-secrets-of-great-communicators/ (archived at perma.cc/CM6H-U7HP)

07

View from the top: Goal setting as a strategic lever for growth

Jonathan Raggett is clear what he wants from a manager: mini-mum time spent in an office creating spreadsheets and other documents. Managers, he says, should be out in the business lead-ing their teams, speaking to customers and delivering a great and consistent experience to these customers.

Now chief executive of the multi-award-winning Red Carnation Collection hotel chain, Jonathan truly knows what it is like to stand in a manager's shoes, having decided that a life of hospitality was for him some three decades ago. He undertook a diploma at Westminster college and joined a management programme, work-ing in different hotels around the world to get as much experience as possible. In 1998 he was appointed general manager at Red Carnation's Rubens and the Palace near Buckingham Palace in London.

A Red Carnation manager meets many guests and makes sure that everything is right for them throughout their whole stay, whether that's one, three or five days. They communicate clearly and need to have energized staff delivering to consistent standards. That's the biggest challenge for any hotel manager: consistency of service. And that is what I want to see Red Carnation managers giving each and every day. I describe it as show business. Every day you come on and you're in front of the crowd and you need to perform.

Red Carnation at a glance

Red Carnation Hotels runs 18 luxury boutique hotels across the world, including six in London, two in Dorset, three in Ireland, one in Scotland, two in the Channel Islands, three in South Africa and one each in Botswana and Switzerland. It is a privately owned business and one of 40 family-owned companies run by The Travel Corporation (TTC). The chain has won multiple awards in the past decade, including being voted number five in The 25 Best Hotel Brands in 2022. Employing 2,500 people, it has also received numerous awards for its people team and as a top employer and its hotels regularly appear in the top five in the TripAdvisor Travellers Choice Awards. Founder and president Beatrice Tollman was voted hotelier of the world by *HOTELS* magazine.

Of course, everyone has a bad day now and again, so maintaining this consistency is not easy, especially when guest expectations are higher than they've ever been and guests are quick to give their feedback on social media and review sites. It's here that goal setting comes in and at Red Carnation this takes the form of well-structured one-to-ones. Every 12 weeks Jonathan meets his managers to discuss their objectives for the next 12 weeks. Managers have ideas, he has his, and they agree together the most important goals. Once the 12 weeks have passed, they review whether they have achieved what they said they would and, if not, why not. They then set out the next 12 weeks' objectives. Importantly, they don't wait until the 12 weeks are up to talk about any issues and challenges preventing them from meeting the objectives.

Jonathan recognizes that there's a fine line to tread to ensure this approach doesn't spill over into micromanagement.

A manager wants to be a manager. They want to be empowered and they want to do their job of work, which I totally get. But one has also got to be very clear about the objectives that are set so that one doesn't go down a path where a manager is doing what they feel is right if it's totally opposed to the idea of what perhaps I, or more importantly the stakeholders, want.

Having as many hotels to look after as I do and having diversity and the global nature of the hotels, I need to have trust in these guys and I need to make sure that I do empower them. And if a week goes by and I don't speak to a general manager, which is rare but can happen, there's no doubt as to what he or she should be doing. We're clear on it. So this isn't about me catching anybody out, it's about how we can go forwards and how we can be aligned. I never want these meetings to be a massive surprise.

This approach has proved successful at Red Carnation, driving good customer service, growth and strong relationships. Many managers have worked with Jonathan for more than 20 years and in the business some team members have been part of the Red Carnation family for more than 60 years. 'When you have that transparency, people know what is expected from them and if you work together effectively you get results,' says Jonathan.

Red Carnation adopts this method throughout the company. Within the hotel teams there are one-to-ones and key performance indicators (KPIs). Systems are in place to make sure these are being done and, if not, teams are asked why. With the variety of people employed by the chain, it can be challenging. This is where good support plays a role. 'For example, we have some great executive chefs who cook well, their health and safety is right up there but sometimes they're not so good at the one-to-ones. So we make sure we give them support to enable them to be comfortable so these can happen. But there can't be any wiggle room because it is proven that you have got to understand your teams and understand where they want to go. It works because we are giving our people these clear objectives.'

Clarity of goal setting aligned to the business and regular conversations also creates an environment for innovation. Ideas are offered and encouraged from the teams. Employee surveys are also used as a tool to understand how people are feeling. 'I don't want miserable staff in the hotel, and it takes a general manager skill set to make sure the team is motivated. They should feel there's a purpose to what they do. And they're enjoying it. Because if you get that part of it right, the rest almost looks after itself – the guest comments and the guest feedback will be positive.'

With general managers responsible for multi-million-pound operations it is important they demonstrate that they know all parts of the business. Jonathan says he wants a manager who's

doing some sales calls, getting out there, who understands housekeeping is tough and spends a day or two per year in that housekeeping department doing the job. Never forget just how tough jobs are, the person who cleans the pots and pans in the kitchen, the person who does the laundry. So let's make sure that we show respect and recognition for these guys.

The worst thing in the world anyone can say to me is, I just do this. For me it's not just 'I am a waiter', 'I am a receptionist'. You are part of this team and it is the team that makes the hotel. I want managers having regular town hall meetings on a monthly basis, recognizing employees. And it's not just words, you have to support people and give them opportunities. If they want to grow from receptionist to a head receptionist to a front house manager, offer the learning development and encourage people.

For me, a general manager adds value by understanding the business and that we need to make sure that we make a profit and we set budgets. But I also want them to enjoy it and have fun. There are times we need to be there and it shouldn't be a chore. It should be because you want to do it, you're part of it, it's in your DNA to be there. It's not for everybody. But if you get excited by hospitality, the giving, making experiences, fulfilling dreams and so on, it's a brilliant career.

TIP
Jonathan's three tips for being a world-class manager

1. Understand every aspect of the business

From marketing to operations, you need to understand every facet of the business. Some people today believe they can fast-track and get there immediately but there isn't a fast-track reality. You need time and patience.

2. Be inquisitive

I read four business books a year. It's vital to keep learning and I challenge my general managers to do this as well. We have a library at Red Carnation where there's a range of books and we swap and share ideas.

3. Be kind but take action

If you want to reach the top in any business, you need to work hard. You need to have energy yourself and to be able to energize others. You need to be driven but you must also care, listen and be kind. You are nothing without a great team. And most of all you must execute on what you say. There's far too much talk, we'll do this and we'll do that, and nothing ever happens. So, to be at the top you've got to have ideas, you've got to get them approved and then you've got to get them done.

08

How to have better meetings for better results

Introduction

Where do most managers in most organizations spend most of their time? With their people? With their customers? In internal meetings? Unfortunately, the answer is almost always the last one. In many cases managers will spend up to two-thirds of their time at work in meetings.

The move to remote working resulting from the pandemic has made the situation worse. According to Microsoft, there was a 252 per cent increase in weekly time spent in meetings and a 153 per cent increase in the number of weekly meetings for the average user of its Teams platform from February 2020 to March 2022.[1] Upwork's Future of Workforce Report 2021 found that changes to the structure and cadence of team meetings forced upon people during the pandemic are management practices that will stay in the long run.[2]

Wherever I go across the world, I hear that meetings are the bane of managers' lives. Too long, too boring, the wrong people attending, dominated by a few people, rambling and passive. Worse still, they are unproductive and wasteful of people's time, with few relevant actions arising. Of managers we've interviewed we've found that only about a third of meetings are seen as useful. Managers say that:

- 70 per cent of people brought other work into meetings
- 39 per cent fell asleep in meetings
- 47 per cent thought the meeting was a just waste of time

Keah Nguyen, senior people specialist at distributed workforce platform company Remote, recognizes the wastefulness. In fact, she says: 'The best way to manage meetings is maybe not to have that meeting at all. Do you really need this meeting? Meetings can be a huge drain on productivity.' Of course, meetings do have their place and at Remote they are clear about when to have a meeting and what they should be used for (see the case study below).

CASE STUDY
Running effective meetings the Remote way

It would probably be wrong if distributed workforce platform company Remote weren't a fully remote business. After all, not only has it nailed its colours to the mast through its name, but its mission is to open up the world of work for every person, business and country.

As such, Remote has more than 930 remote employees across 65 countries and in some 15 time zones. It has been operating this way since it was founded by Job van der Voort and Marcelo Lebre in 2019. So, managers at Remote know a thing or two about asynchronous work, that is, work that is not time-bound and reliant on a team member to be available at the same time.

Working this way means conversations normally take place via messaging platform Slack, note-taking software Notion or work management platform Asana. Whatever time zone Remote's people are in, they can come on to platforms such as these and catch up with everything that has happened in the past 12 hours.

This, says senior people specialist Keah Nguyen, means 90 per cent of problems are solved asynchronously, so teams only 'sync' in meetings once a week, much of which is spent socially connecting and team bonding. But before any meeting is convened a manager should ask whether it is needed at all. This avoids getting to the stage of 'Zoom fatigue' where everyone is spending all day in meetings staring at a screen. Second, with a globally distributed team, it can be difficult to bring all of the time zones together at the same time. At Remote, meetings are not used for information sharing, because there are so many other ways to do this.

> When I think about how we work together, we get so much done efficiently and with great transparency because work doesn't happen in a meeting, it happens publicly in a Slack channel, for example, so anyone can contribute at any time. This means there should be really good reasons why you are having a meeting, such as where there's a lot of back and forth to discuss a project, to enforce shared values or to break bottlenecks.

When there is this need for a meeting the first action is to prepare an agenda. As Keah says: 'A meeting without an agenda is like driving to a new location where you don't have the directions, so you'll get there eventually but you'll probably get lost on the way. It will take you longer and you will be more stressed.' The agenda is editable so everyone can contribute to it.

Meetings are recorded, and topics raised and decisions made are documented. Best practice at Remote is that everyone who isn't talking can document it. Meetings are kept to 25 minutes instead of 30 minutes, to give five minutes at the end to clean up notes or to re-centre before the next activity.

After the meeting the recording and documentation are shared publicly within the organization so that those who were not at the meeting can see what was being discussed and the decisions that came out of it. This enables people to collaborate and comment even if they were unable to attend and also ensures inclusivity.

Running effective meetings is clearly a challenge. More than three-quarters (78.1 per cent) of the managers surveyed said they felt they could make their meetings more effective and nearly 4 in 10 (39.3 per cent) do not believe they have made sure their team always leaves a meeting with clarity and actions.

World-class managers know how to make the time spent in meetings count. They create meetings that people want to attend because their meetings have value for everyone who attends.

There are three essential elements to ensuring a meeting adds value:

1 **Preparation.** From concise and relevant agendas to the dynamics of attendees, preparation is key. The more time we spend on this part of it, the shorter the meeting needs to be.

2 **Execution.** A well-chaired meeting is orderly and feels like a good use of time. People get the say they want and decisions or choices are made.

3 **Follow-up.** What you do after is as important as what you do before and during the meeting.

Here is how you can make an impact in meetings, starting today.

The WCM 7

- Make sure you prepare well.
- Create an agenda and invite others to contribute to it.
- Get off to a good start.
- Establish the ground rules and manage behaviours.
- Create a positive energy in the room.
- End with action points.
- Follow up in a timely fashion.

1. Make sure you prepare well

Whether you are the leader or the participant in a meeting, think about some key questions to ask well in advance of the meeting taking place. These should include:

- What is the purpose of the meeting – what are the topics and why are you holding the meeting?
- Is the meeting necessary – could another form of communication, such as email, be a better use of time?
- What is the desired outcome?
- Who needs to be there?
- What is the best format to have a useful and action-focused discussion?
- What is the best role that you can play – how can you enhance your impact in the way you 'show up' in the meeting?

2. Create an agenda and invite others to contribute to it

It's important to pull together an agenda and, if appropriate, get other key people to contribute to it. This will get people more engaged in the meeting and should lead to a better outcome. When time is so precious, getting everyone focused around the agenda and what you are all trying to achieve is vital.

Consider the following for inclusion in the agenda:

- List material people should read in advance of the meeting.
- Have clear meeting objectives.
- List the agenda topics and tasks.
- Start with topics that can be quickly resolved to create a positive energy.
- Establish the responsibilities and expectations for those involved.
- Estimate a realistic timescale for each task.
- Share the agenda at least 24 hours before the meeting.

Figure 8.1   Agree agenda

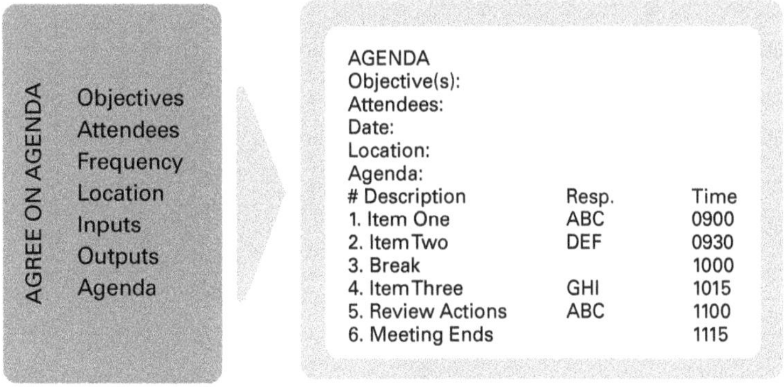

AGREE ON AGENDA

Objectives
Attendees
Frequency
Location
Inputs
Outputs
Agenda

```
AGENDA
Objective(s):
Attendees:
Date:
Location:
Agenda:
# Description          Resp.      Time
1. Item One            ABC        0900
2. Item Two            DEF        0930
3. Break                          1000
4. Item Three          GHI        1015
5. Review Actions      ABC        1100
6. Meeting Ends                   1115
```

3. Get off to a good start

Make sure the meeting starts on time and has a positive tone right from the beginning. Begin with statements such as:

'I'd like to welcome everyone.'

'I'd like to thank everyone for coming today.'

'I appreciate your attending today.'

Keep your introduction short and to the point. Include a reminder of why the meeting is taking place, what you are trying to achieve and what you are looking for from the participants. This will reiterate that there is a clear purpose and that the results will have impact. If you do not set the scene effectively it can lead to a lack of focus and will not get the best out of the session.

Try to avoid using 'I' and instead use 'we' throughout the meeting. This will help participants feel ownership of any outcomes. It is good to practise your introduction before the meeting. Consider your tone of voice and body language.

4. Establish the ground rules and manage behaviours

We all want healthy debate in meetings and to get our best ideas on to the table to help us make the best decisions we can for the good of the enterprise. However, bad behaviours, or disrespectful challenging, can be destructive and create a negative meetings culture in which people may not feel safe to participate fully.

Our research found that some of the bad behaviours experienced in meetings are people having side conversations and people who talk too much and dominate the meeting. However, 70.8 per cent of managers do not challenge these bad behaviours during meetings.

World-class managers do challenge these behaviours to ensure they get the best possible outcomes from meetings – not just for the project in hand but also for the culture of the organization. As the meetings leader, try to keep any negative behaviours in check and focus people on the positive outcomes you are all trying to achieve. Your leadership will ultimately define the meetings culture in your team.

TIP
How to deal with challenging behaviours

The person who talks too much

If someone is talking too much, respectfully acknowledge their contribution, but say that you would like input from others before we can all make a decision.

Side conversations

Gently remind those having a side conversation of what you are trying to do and that you would value their thoughts on what you are all discussing.

The person who doesn't say anything

Try gently asking directly for their opinion, or compliment and encourage them the first time they talk. It is important to create an environment where people feel safe to give their point of view and where everyone in the room feels valued.

Cynics and naysayers

Acknowledge their complaints but emphasize that you are all here to try and find better ways of doing things by constructive collaboration. The plan is to shift their thinking to a more positive place.

Egos

I'm sure we've all met people with strong egos. People's egos can be challenging, particularly if they feel strongly about a point. One way to deal with them is to compliment them on their passion and their contribution, acknowledge the points that you all agree on, and emphasize that it would be great to try to find a constructive solution to the issue being discussed.

Good luck! Managing people's behaviours is not easy but if you can be seen as someone who is always looking for a positive outcome and keeps negativity at bay, it will really enhance your brand as a leader.

5. Create a positive energy in the room

How many meetings have you been to where the energy is almost on the floor and there is no spark in the discussion? People appreciate positive energizers – there are far too many mood hoovers out there and they need to be counterbalanced!

Think about your tone of voice, body language and speed of delivery. Consider which tone is most appropriate for the meeting topic and how you want to come across:

- Motivating tone
- Humorous tone
- Formal tone
- Serious tone
- Assertive tone
- Informal tone
- Optimistic tone
- Respectful tone

Watch your body language. Non-verbal communication such as your posture and gestures can affect the message you are communicating, how trustworthy you are seen to be by your people and how engaged they are in your message. Despite what is coming from your mouth, your body language may be giving out different signals. For example, hunched shoulders, lack of eye contact and crossed arms can look defensive. Hands on hips appear aggressive. On the other hand, good eye contact, positive gestures, smiling and nodding in agreement are engaging.

6. End with action points

A bad meeting is one that has no clear outcomes or actions, fizzles out listlessly and does not lead to anything worthwhile, let alone any action. Good meetings have a clarity and focus where there are agreed actions and next steps.

World-class managers focus meetings on the outcomes, not on how long it takes to discuss an issue. Don't block your meetings into a specific amount of time for each element. But do make sure the meeting ends on time! People can get tremendously frustrated by meetings that overrun.

Make sure you end the meeting by reviewing and summarizing key action points. Try to pull out the three most important. Ask if everyone is clear and give time for people who have lingering concerns to raise them. Agree on next steps. This closes the meeting with everyone aligned and ensures progress will be made. It is easy for people to leave a meeting with different interpretations of what was agreed and even discussed.

And to keep people in a positive frame of mind, why not add five minutes where you give a shout out to people present who have achieved something positive – inside or outside the organization.

7. Follow up

Follow up as soon as possible with an email that summarizes the key points, agreed actions and next steps, and who will do what and by when. Include the next meeting date if appropriate.

Conclusion

Great meetings do lead to better results but, as we have seen, all too often managers' calendars can be filled with meetings from beginning to end of day that are not moving anything of value forward. Unstructured meetings without a clear agenda and purpose are at best a waste of time and at worst actively disengaging participants and preventing them from using that time to actively benefit the organization.

In today's agile organization, meetings are not confined to the conference room with 30 people in attendance. In his description of the characteristics of what he calls an 'Irresistible' organization, analyst Josh Bersin talks about today's work environment featuring many small meeting areas, for more targeted meetings or regular recognition or social events.[3] Your organization may not be able to go as far as outdoor clothing brand Patagonia, which regularly has employee meetings at the beach with people wearing casual clothes and being encouraged to surf but perhaps you could conduct a walking meeting with one of your team members like health insurance company Aetna does, or hold 15-minute stand-up meetings to improve wellbeing at the same time.[4]

World-class managers run effective meetings that end with actions adding value to the organization. So before you hold your next meeting, be it with your team, other people in the organization or your customer, be sure to re-read this chapter to get the best out of it.

CHECKLIST
Actions to take now

- Review your calendar. How many meetings are you attending per week? How many are essential for you to attend? Are you getting what you need from these meetings to make you and your team more effective? Try to remove meetings that do not move you forward to your goals.

- Experiment. Try different meeting lengths and formats. Could you bring in guest speakers or ask one of your team to chair the meeting to keep the format fresh?

- Analyse your own performance in meetings. Consider it both from the perspective of leading the meeting and participating in it. Write down the opportunities for you to increase your impact.

Notes

1 Microsoft (2022) Work Trend Index Special Report. www.microsoft.com/en-us/worklab/work-trend-index (archived at perma.cc/C9QS-3CJV)
2 Upwork (2021) Future Workforce Report 2021: How remote work is changing business forever. www.upwork.com/research/future-workforce-report/ (archived at perma.cc/C6SV-PYBY)
3 Bersin, J (2022) *Irresistible: The seven secrets of the world's most enduring, employee-focused organizations.* Vicara Books, Wood Dale, IL

4 The Washington Post (2014) A Company That Profits as it Pampers Workers. www.washingtonpost.com/business/a-company-that-profits-as-it-pampers-workers/2014/10/22/d3321b34-4818-11e4-b72e-d60a9229cc10_story.html (archived at perma.cc/2CP7-3YEE)

09

The importance of understanding your customer

Introduction

'The purpose of business is to create and keep a customer,' stated legendary management educator Peter Drucker.[1] The purpose of a manager, therefore, is to ensure that the customer is satisfied and loyal through understanding what they want and providing the tools and support to team members so that they can deliver exceptional customer service.

A manager's customer can be external, the buyer or user of the service/product provided by the organization, or internal, for example other departments and people in the case of functions such as HR, IT or finance.

The good news is that our research found 97.4 per cent of managers say they care about their customers' experiences, 82.8 per cent say they share good or bad feedback with their team and 74.3 per cent say they are always looking for new ways and ideas to keep customers happy.

The bad news is that other research suggests managers generally fail to understand their organization's customers. They systematically overestimate the levels of customer satisfaction and attitudinal loyalty, and their understanding of the drivers of their customers' satisfaction and loyalty are disconnected from those of their actual customers.

The American Customer Satisfaction Index (ACSI) research found that managers tend to underestimate the importance both of customer perceptions of quality in driving their satisfaction and of the role of satisfaction in driving customers' loyalty and complaint behaviour.[2]

Meanwhile, a study by Adweek and Accenture found that 80 per cent of companies believe they deliver a superior customer service, but only 8 per cent of customers agree.[3]

Why is this important? Well, most companies rely heavily on repeat business. It's therefore vital that a business has satisfied customers or else they will go elsewhere. So, managers need to know what their customers think of their product and service offerings. And they need to ensure that their teams are delivering exceptional customer service.

Companies are increasingly waking up to the fact that customer experience is dependent on employee experience. In a survey of 655 decision makers and influencers in business and IT conducted by IDC, 85 per cent agreed that an improved employee experience and higher employee engagement translate to a better customer experience, higher customer satisfaction and higher revenues for their organization. More than 6 in 10 (62 per cent) went as far as to say there is a defined causal relationship between employee experience (EX) and customer experience (CX) and described the impact of that relationship as 'large' or 'significant'.[4]

The challenge is that customer expectations have changed greatly over the past few years and people now expect a lot more from you and your team. In our 'always on' world, customers expect to be able to engage with your product or service whenever they want on whichever channel they want. They expect you to respond in the same way. They expect you to offer more personal communication at a time that suits them.

A separate piece of research from Accenture reveals that 88 per cent of executives think their customers are changing faster than their businesses can keep up and 64 per cent of consumers wish companies would respond faster to meet their changing needs.[5] Meanwhile, research by Big 4 consultancy PwC found 82 per cent of US and 74 per cent of non-US consumers want more human interaction in the future but 59 per cent feel that companies have lost touch with the human element of customer experience. Worse still, only 38 per cent of US consumers and 46 per cent of those outside the United States say employees whom they do interact with understand their needs.[6]

If you fail to satisfy these customers, your organization – and possibly you personally – could very well be faced with negative reviews all over the web and social media. And, of course, you can lose their business. Global communications group Havas has produced its Meaningful Brand Report since 2009. Its latest survey of 395,000 consumers found that an astonishing 75 per cent of brands could disappear and most customers wouldn't care or would easily find a replacement.[7]

World-class managers can identify and resolve issues that are causing customers to leave, while also finding ways of keeping customers happy and loyal in the future. They have empathy for the people they serve, by which I mean the ability to see things through the customer's eyes. Organizations can hold huge amounts of data and insights as to what their customers want, but world-class managers challenge this to get to the real truths. After all, what people say is not always what they really want. And by the time the data gets into your hands it may have already been distorted.

World-class managers also create the right customer-centric culture within their team. It's about designing and delivering an experience where your customers feel you care for them. This may sound soft, but it's one of the biggest drivers of whether or not a customer will come back to you a second time. Indeed, our research found that 68.3 per cent of managers say they provide their team with the tools and support to deliver an exceptional service to the customer. We look at this in more detail later in this chapter.

Of course, it all begins with understanding whom we're serving and what they want. There are three key things to think about here:

1 Are we still delivering what our customers want? This question is valid, whether you are talking about external or internal customers. It's a great test question, as it's easy to make assumptions here without considering changing customer expectations. World-class managers continually check.

2 Are we future focused? As noted above, understanding the changing trends and landscape that are impacting our customers' 'world' is key to being able to better predict how their challenges will change and how we can best deliver on what they want, now and tomorrow.

3 Are we upping our game? As the saying goes, if you're not moving forwards then you're moving backwards. We know that people are always looking to go one better, to do it faster, cheaper, with more style, for a better reason/purpose. World-class managers keep looking at how to improve the experience external customers have of dealing with us and our teams. The same applies internally. If you don't focus on continuous improvement, it's a fast way to damage your career prospects.

It's important that everyone in your team shares a common mission related to the customer, and your role is to ensure this is the case. This is especially important in today's VUCA (volatile, uncertain, complex and ambiguous) world where creative problem solving is required. All the scripts, processes, training and rules cannot help when customers have such unique and fast-changing needs. Having a clear customer-centric mission provides the boundaries when a quick decision is required.

So, what actions can you take to make an impact? Here's what we have discovered to be the core steps taken by world-class managers when it comes to the customer.

The WCM 7

- Be a role model to your team.
- Be clear on your role in the customer service chain.
- Spend time with your customers.
- Ensure your team has the right tools and support.
- Share customer feedback with the team.
- Keep improving.
- Try to stay one step ahead.

1. Be a role model to your team

Great managers demonstrate a true customer service mindset. They always aim for excellence in service delivery. They look to continuously improve that service. They get close to their customers to understand them better. As a leader, you set the standard – if you show passion for customers your team will follow.

Check against the framework shown in Figure 9.1 to ensure you are seen as a role model in your team.

Professionalism

Great role models hold themselves, and their work, to the highest standards. Being responsible shows that you're aware of what your role actually entails and that you're ready to be held accountable for your actions and the results they produce. If you remain professional, even when times get tough, your team will follow suit.

Trust

A role model manager must be trustworthy. Your team will not show any respect if you aren't honest. Be consistent in your honesty and your team will see it.

Figure 9.1 Role-modelling framework

Integrity

Working with integrity means doing the right thing for the right reasons, even if it isn't the easy choice. In return, your team will respect you and your decisions and they will operate with the values that you require.

Strive for improvement

Being an expert in your field helps when you are role modelling. This attribute shows that you value improvement and want to be the most effective employee and team member you can be. Always try to find new and more effective ways of doing things, involve your team and ask for their input.

Morality and ethics

This can mean different things depending on the sector in which you work but generally means identifying which moral codes you should be following. In order to understand your own workplace morality and ethics, you should read your company procedures and policies and speak with your colleagues and peers about it.

Positive attitude (always)

Positivity breeds positivity while negative behaviour can spread to those around you. As a manager, always try to keep things positive when delivering messages or discussing any projects that you are working on, even if you may not feel that way about it inside. The team must always feel that you are behind whatever message or project you are focusing on.

Empathy

Take time to listen to those around you, try to see things from their perspective but also offer guidance as to how they could work around any issues or problems they may have. This can-do attitude will set you up to be a great role model for your people and organization.

2. Be clear on your role in the customer service chain

You will either be serving customers directly or serving someone who serves the customer. So how clear are you about their expectations and of what excellence looks like in their eyes? Great managers take the time to find out if they are meeting their customers' expectations and how they might make their service even better.

If you are serving an internal customer, you will need to ensure you work cohesively with all areas of your organization. As a manager, try to bust the siloed working that many organizations have. As Kathleen Schaub, adviser to marketing leaders, said in an article in CMSWire: 'When your entire organization has a siloed view of customer experience, the mission is lost and customers pay the price.'[8]

Whenever possible, suggest colleagues from another department in the organization spend the day in your department or team – and swap one of your team into the other department. Following these experience days, ask the individual to share feedback on what they have seen and heard during their time in that department, discuss what works well and what could be improved.

Improving our internal customer services leads to us being able to cut costs, increase productivity, improve communication, boost morale and therefore deliver better service to our external customers.

If your customer is an external customer, you will need to review your organization's values and provide your customer service based on those values. For example, if one of your organizational values is empathy, you should try to show empathy and understanding in all of your customer interactions. If your customer is making a complaint, maybe spend some time speaking with them to understand how they are feeling and why they may not be happy with the service or product they received compared to what they were expecting. By living the values of the organization, you will be truly aligned to what your organization is trying to achieve.

3. Spend time with your customers

We would recommend that you spend time with your customers and get to know them better. Find out what's important to them. What are their goals and ambitions? What frustrates them? What are their pain points and how can you help them be even more successful? Doing this will give you ideas and insights and will help you improve your service to them. It will also strengthen your relationship with them.

Try using some the questions below to get into the mindset of your customers:

- Tell me about yourself and why you chose us.
- How satisfied are you with our products/services?
- On a scale of 1 to 10, how happy are you with our product?
- Why did you give us that score?
- Can you explain the weaknesses or challenges you've found in our product/service so far?
- What do you love about our product/service?
- What can my company do to better serve your needs?
- What value do we provide?
- What are your biggest challenges when dealing with us?
- Why did you choose us over the competition? What are the main reasons you chose to go ahead with us today?
- How did you feel about our customer service?
- Where did you look before coming to us?
- Would you use our product/service again?
- What did you like best about your experience?

4. Tools and support

Does your team have the tools and support they need to deliver great service? How often do you sit down with your team to test this? Great managers we meet regularly have these kinds of discussions with their teams and they act on any feedback.

If your team members are stressed or unhappy, how can you expect them to deliver good service to the customer? According to a survey from WebEx by Cisco and CMSWire, 47 per cent of managers said workloads were the primary cause for poor customer service.[9] If you are not looking after your people, they will not look after your customers.

As a manager, you should be offering ongoing training and development for new and existing employees on aspects related to customer service. Training on topics such as negotiating skills or phone-handling skills will always be beneficial for your team. If your organization does not have any budget to provide official training, see if you can put a training programme together yourself from your past knowledge or look out for articles or free courses online that can give your people the support and guidance they need.

You can also try knowledge-sharing sessions with your colleagues and peers. This is another cost-effective way to discuss experiences and come up with solutions to improve the service or product that you provide.

All organizations have rules and guidelines on how to operate, but as a manager you should create a culture of encouraging your people to solve problems where they can. Empower them with the authority and flexibility to find creative or alternative solutions to issues when they arise, without having to get your sign-off on every little thing. Giving them this autonomy is a confidence boost to your people.

As in other areas, listening plays a major role in supporting your people with customer service. Your team need to feel comfortable bringing you information about problems that have occurred, asking questions or making suggestions for improvement. I discussed how to develop listening skills in Chapter 4 on appraisals.

5. Share customer feedback with the team

Everyone loves to hear that their efforts are making a difference. How often and how effectively do you share positive customer feedback with your team?

You can collect customer feedback via customer or employee engagement surveys, social media or online reviews. If you do not have a feedback channel already, you will need to set up an effective way to gather that feedback. Even if the feedback is sent by email, company intranet or post, it is essential to have a flow of feedback comments. Do you have effective channels in place for your customers to provide real-time feedback on your products and services and their experience? Do you have your email address at the bottom of your signature or newsletters where customers can send you feedback?

Share all feedback – good and bad – if you want to improve the service or product that you provide. When sharing feedback, you will need to avoid blaming individuals when reviewing negative feedback. Take the feedback as a way to improve and do things differently.

And celebrate the positivity – this will encourage your people to continue doing what works well. One client we worked with in the hospitality sector has daily WOW sessions to share customer feedback. These help to build pride, generate positivity and reinforce the values of the organization. Another great tip is to do some public relations. Let others in the business know when you do receive positive feedback. It is good PR for you and your team.

6. Keep improving

Top managers don't just have a great handle on what customers want, they also have a sense of what they will want next. So many famous leaders, from Apple founder Steve Jobs to architect Denys Lasdun, have described their desire to give their customers something they haven't even thought about. That's pure customer delight.

Constantly review your delivery and work with the team to improve your service. Great managers actively involve their teams and their customers to generate new ideas.

Global analyst and founder of Bersin by Deloitte Josh Bersin tells a great story that illustrates how harnessing your people's knowledge of customers can positively impact the business. The power tools division of global technology and services giant Bosch is a world leader in the design, manufacture and sale of power tools and accessories. Like many businesses, it organized its model around the products it was selling. However, margins were going down, competition was rising and it had to find a way to digitize the business. So, it turned to its sales and engineering team and asked how they thought it could better organize. And those people said: 'We're not really in the business of selling drills. We're in the business of making holes. And, from there, we're not really in the business of making holes. We're in the business of helping people build things. So maybe we ought to organize around what our customers are trying to do, not what the products are that we are trying to sell.'

On the back of this, Bosch redesigned the product and marketing function around the engineering and construction problems its customers wanted to solve – and then looked at the products, tools and engineering needed to solve these problems. The result? Productivity, market share and revenue all increased.[10]

7. Try to stay one step ahead

Steve Jobs' famous quote, 'get close to your customer, so close that you tell them what they need, even before they realize it themselves', is so relevant in today's fast-paced, competitive world.[11] We see great managers being proactive in this area – they go to their customers with new ideas that create value for the customer. Is this something you do, or could you do more of it? Here are some places to start.

Ask customers for their improvement ideas

To stay a step ahead of your customers, try to listen to feedback regarding anything that did not hit the mark with your customers. Always ask customers and clients what you could have done to make the process or service better. They may give you some suggestions that you have never thought of before.

Don't forget about existing customers

We can all be too focused on attracting new customers, but it's our existing customers that are most likely to give you real feedback on what's working, what's not, and what could be done differently. Try to make the most of your existing relationships before you start trying to find new ones.

Review your competition

You should regularly review what your competition is doing and what are they offering. Are you competitive on price and keeping up to date with technology and product design? Are your competitors offering additional services? Identify any areas that you can change things to compete. It is a great way to enhance your reputation and to strengthen the customer relationship.

Conclusion

It's never been more important to connect deeply with your customers. Loyalty to brands is declining and customers crave an emotional connection to organizations they do business with or from whom they purchase. While technology has made reaching customers and dealing with complaints easier, as we found at the beginning of this chapter, it is human interaction that so many of your customers desire. World-class managers ensure that this human interaction is positive and leaves the customer feeling good.

Of course, none of this can happen if you don't have a great team which truly understands what the organization is trying to achieve and marries that with the customer experience they are giving or innovations they suggest. So, in the next chapter we will take a look at what makes a world-class team.

Chapter review

Questions for reflection

As you consider your role as a world-class manager, reflect on the following questions and capture them in a way that works for you. Write notes, start a journal, record on your phone or capture on a spreadsheet – whichever will enable you to remember these points when dealing with your team and other people in your organization.

- Do you fully understand your customer's needs and expectations?
- How well do you engage with them?
- How well do you seek and share feedback from customers with your team?
- How proactive are you in bringing new ideas to your customers?
- What are the opportunity areas for you to enhance your impact with your customers – external or internal?

Actions to take now

- Interview at least three customers either personally or over the phone if face-to-face isn't possible. Ask them what they think of the service/product they get from your team.
- Ask what you can do to better understand their needs (either quantifiably like Net Promoter Score or qualitatively through

focus groups). What can we 'do' to make the service/product we offer even better?

- Plan for three years ahead. Given what you know about your customers and their world, what is likely to be different in three years? Write it down.

Notes

1 Cohen, W (2012) *Drucker on Marketing: Lessons from the world's most influential business thinker.* McGraw-Hill, *New York*

2 ACSI 70,000 American Customer Satisfaction Index (ACSI) Customer Surveys and 1,068 Firm (Manager) Responses From the ACSI-Measured Companies

3 Shah, B, Barton, R, Van der Ouderaa, E and Bjornsjo, A (2022) The Human Paradox: From customer centricity to life centricity. www.accenture.com/_acnmedia/PDF-180/Accenture-Human-Paradox.pdf#zoom=40 (archived at perma.cc/TEZ5-865A)

4 IDC (2021) Relating Employee Experience to Customer Experience. www.idc.com/getdoc.jsp?containerId=US48114321 (archived at perma.cc/SWH7-E292)

5 Accenture What is Customer Experience? And Why it's Evolving. www.accenture.com/us-en/insights/song/customer-experience-index (archived at perma.cc/M7K4-ZP4Y)

6 PwC (2018) Experience is Everything. Get it Right. www.pwc.com/us/en/services/consulting/library/consumer-intelligence-series/future-of-customer-experience.html (archived at perma.cc/W8JB-5LLY)

7 Havas (2021) Meaningful Brands Report. www.meaningful-brands.com (archived at perma.cc/PT8Q-3C6Q)

8 Schaub, K (2022) Customer-Centric Missions Keep Frontlines Prepared for the Unexpected. www.cmswire.com/customer-experience/customer-centric-missions-keep-frontlines-prepared-for-the-unexpected (archived at perma.cc/8B2N-ATE3)

9 Webex by Cisco (nd) Supercharge Customer Experiences Through Great Agent Support. webexahead.webex.com/supercharge-customer-experiences-through-great-agent-support/ (archived at perma.cc/URX4-X4WQ)

10 Bersin, J (2022) Irresistible By Design: The winning strategy for the future. joshbersin.com/2022/06/irresistible-by-design-the-winning-strategy-for-the-future/ (archived at perma.cc/46Y6-XEUX)

11 So, C (2020) 5 Lessons Steve Jobs Can Teach You About Proposal Management. goraft.tech/2020/04/23/5-lessons-steve-jobs-can-teach-you-about-proposal-management.html (archived at perma.cc/X2QU-GD4C)

10
How to create a standout team

Introduction

When Ian Ashcroft arrived to lead a human resources team at a well-known international publishing company, he was flummoxed. Back in the 1990s every Friday a fax machine ground away for four hours while the team sat at their computers. He asked what was going on. 'It's all the absentee and holiday requests coming in,' said one team member. 'We put them in hanging files.' For what purpose, asked Ian? 'So that if an employee at the end of the year says they have six days' holiday left and their manager thinks it is only three, they will ring us up and we will rummage through the files and confirm the number of days remaining.'

Ian had stumbled into a scenario we see time and again in organizations. Here was a team full of bright talented people who could deliver so much to the company but who in reality were 'just doing jobs'. There was no joined-up thinking, no credibility for the department in the business and the team was not adding value. Worse still, one manager was actively undermining the value of the team. Because they didn't like one employee, they brought in external people for £800 a time to do what that employee could do as part of their salary. And this manager used to shout at their assistant rather than get up from their chair and walk the few steps to speak to them.

It was quickly clear that we needed lots of change. I had to make some difficult decisions regarding whether we had the right people in place. Once that was done, I said to the team, 'You tell me how we improve things for yourselves and the department – and therefore for the business.' And they came back with a plan whereby they released more than 20 per cent of their time to focus on more value-adding work. I gave them the opportunity to own their jobs, to control their own destiny to some extent. And guess what? They reacted 100 per cent positively. And then we presented the changes back to the business and they were accepted. From that day on, we were seen as delivering real value to the company.

Ian's story highlights the challenges of running a team and why managers who create high-performing teams are so in demand. You can't just put a group of highly talented people together and hope they form a productive and cohesive group. As manager, it is your role to intentionally build and maintain the team so that the whole performs better than the individuals it comprises. High-performing teams stand out for all the right reasons. They have great team cultures, clear visions and distinct responsibilities. They're teams people want to work in, teams where people thrive and teams that deliver real value to their organizations.

World-class managers know that every team has potential and that they are the catalyst to harnessing that potential. Everyone wants to get better at what they do, no matter what it is that they do. A culture of high performance, built in the right way, is key to creating openings for people to develop and grow.

Unfortunately, in research we have done with 628 managers globally we have discovered there is still some way to go to become truly world-class when it comes to creating high-performing teams. Just 6 in 10 managers say they often take a step back and look for any improvements and 68 per cent that they consistently empower their team. And while nearly 78 per cent say they always translate key messages to their team and 81 per cent that they are focused on creating a great culture for their team, that leaves around a fifth of managers who do not do these vital activities.

As a world-class manager, you are in a vital leadership position and you are the CEO's best shot at translating strategic messages in a way that means something to your team, as you have the closest relationship with them. You have the chance to create a team that people want to be a part of – and a team that those outside of it want to be part of. In every organization there is that one team that's perceived as the best, the one everyone talks highly about and the one that looks like it has the most fun.

This is an opportunity for your team to make an impact on the business that's greater than the sum of its parts because team members understand how to harness their skills, talent and drive. Combine this with the knowledge of how their role helps hit key targets and you have a powerful mix.

As a manager your team is your brand. So, if you can create a standout team that is perceived as a standout in the business, you can make a big difference – to overall performance and to your own profile. So, let's look at how you can do that.

The WCM 7

- Have a clear sense of what world-class looks like in your team.
- Ensure there is job clarity.
- Focus on measurement.
- Ditch micromanagement and empower your team.
- Maintain high levels of performance.
- Celebrate and recognize success.
- Be a role model.

1. Have a clear sense of what world-class looks like in your team

All high-performing teams have a clear sense of purpose – something that defines them, something they want to be known for.

It may be exceptional service delivery, increased innovation or high achievement. Whatever the purpose, they want to stand out. Typically, in world-class organizations we find a leader who is ambitious and driven but also team members who share their passion for success. That leader sets the bar high with ambitious goals, wanting everyone to be the best they can be.

Take some time with your team to brainstorm ideas as to what being world-class feels like for them. Ask them to think about the following items:

- What does world-class mean to them?
- What kind of product or service would you and your team produce if you were world-class?
- What support, finance, technology or additional resources do you and your team need to be world-class?
- What are the things that will block you and your team from being world-class?
- What do your competitors do that make them seem like they are world-class?

Once you have brainstormed these types of questions, you should be able to work through the common themes to get an idea of what your team wants to achieve and how you are going to do it. Once you have established what your world-class looks like, agree on a timescale and try to work backwards on how you will achieve this standard.

2. Ensure there is job clarity

It is impossible to have a high-performing team when people are not clear on their roles and responsibilities. Everyone needs to know what is expected of them, and your role as a manager is to make this clear. Making sure your team has a clear understanding of their individual responsibilities, tasks and processes as well as those of their colleagues is therefore vital if you are to create a standout team.

Research has found that role ambiguity creates tension and anxiety among employees and reduces their productivity. A study of small and medium-sized IT companies in India found that when employees know what is expected of their role they tend to perform better. Role clarity improved job satisfaction and, in turn, job performance.[1] The authors note that role ambiguity is considered to be one of the great bottlenecks for team effectiveness, while role conflict – having different and incompatible roles at the same time – causes employee stress.

Meanwhile, a study by one of Europe's largest employee feedback solutions providers, Effectory, found 86 per cent of employees with high role clarity report high levels of effectiveness, 84 per cent report high intention to stay and 75 per cent high satisfaction in leadership.[2] Our own research with 1,324 managers globally found 63.6 per cent feel they are completely clear about what is expected of them in their role. But if you are one of the 36 per cent who are not therefore clear, are you giving clarity to your team?

We've seen some high-performing teams create their own charters of the key behaviours that will make them successful – something similar to team values. They publicize these expectations and make them visible to all to create a high degree of ownership.

To give your team job clarity you should do the following:

- Set SMART goals for the team and align them to the organization (see Chapter 2 'Great goal setting').
- Set boundaries that everyone stays within.
- Ask your team members regularly for their ideas (and acknowledge those ideas with your peers).
- Explain how the tasks and duties they carry out on a day-to-day basis contribute to the organization's vision and mission.
- Assign tasks with appropriate measurement.

3. Focus on measurement

High-performing managers are fanatical about measurement. They create rigorous KPIs to help them monitor performance. They use data, research and feedback to help them review and constantly adjust their team's performance. The old saying 'you can't achieve what you can't measure' is as true today as it ever was – and even more so in the world of big data. World-class managers use this to their advantage.

There are different ways that you can set measurements for you and your team. If you don't have them in place already you could consider the following measurements:

- Customer satisfaction rating
- Employee engagement level
- Business growth
- Business profitability

As a team you could also measure:

- Quality of work
- Commitment
- Working efficiency and streamlining
- Innovation
- Displaying teamwork

To be able to put these measurements in place you will need to:

1 Set metrics for every project or task.

2 Check in regularly.

3 Set realistic goals and targets.

4. Ditch micromanagement and empower your team

There was a great thread on Twitter in which people were asked to describe a time that they had worked for a micromanager without saying these actual words. The responses were as amusing as you would expect, ranging from 'he checks my tweets so best I don't respond' and 'bringing a gavel to senior leadership team meetings' to 'sends email and then comes up to me five minutes later asking about said email'. Even those who didn't give an example recognized the typical signs of micromanagement. It was one of those threads you read and say, oh yes!

Micromanagement in organizations is persistent. Workplace researcher and consultant Corporate Rebels calls it 'Corporate disease No.1'. Co-founder Pim de Morree says it's as persistent as a mosquito you can never seem to swat away and argues it is the default approach for many managers.[3] Anyone who has been micromanaged will recognize how true this analogy is. Have you ever come across someone who enjoys being micromanaged? Of course not.

Micromanagement can lead to disengagement and a stifling of creativity. World-class managers empower, not micromanage. Key to this is a high degree of trust, allowing people the space to get on with their jobs while also feeling supported by their manager and colleagues. Trust is foundational to building a high-performing team. This became starkly clear during the pandemic where many employees worked autonomously and remotely for the first time. Research by academics Sharon Parker, Caroline Knight and Anita Keller published in *Harvard Business Review* in 2020 found that many managers were struggling with managing people effectively at home – and this translated into micromanagement and workers feeling untrusted.[4]

Empowering your team requires delegation skills. I'm reminded of a question asked by Chris Roebuck, a leadership speaker who was appointed honorary visiting professor of transformational leadership at Bayes Business School in 2009, at a conference I attended back in 2018. He asked the assembled managers and leaders to put their hands in the air if they had ever been formally trained to delegate on a day-to-day basis. No one did. He has asked that question many times across the world and there are never more than 25 per cent of people who put their hands up. No wonder managers are so often complaining about lack of time to achieve their goals!

We have a simple framework you can use to decide when to delegate and to whom. First, analyse the tasks you and your team need to deliver and create a priorities list. Then put them into three categories:

- The standard to which the end-product needs to be delivered
- The skills and experience level needed
- The time and effort needed

Follow this by considering which tasks only you can do and which tasks could be designated. When deciding who on your team is best placed to take on that task, ask the following questions:

- What are their skills and experience level?
- What are their development needs and wants?
- What does the organization need?
- How could delegation benefit succession planning and team strength?
- What exposure would it give that team member?
- What time is available to complete the task?
- How much support will you have to give that team member in terms of guidance and coaching?
- Will they need any additional training?

A useful framework we use to determine how much direction or empowerment suits that employee is the Skill Will Matrix (Figure 10.1).

Figure 10.1   The Skill/Will Matrix

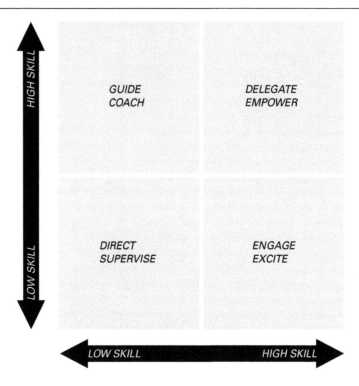

Think about where you would plot each team member on the grid.

High Will/Low Skill

If they are willing but lacking in skills, you need to provide more guidance, coaching and teaching. This person may be motivated but will need your guidance to support and deliver.

Low Will/Low Skill

Identify any blockers that may be causing the lower will and be ready to direct and supervise more closely. You will need to set clear expectations, closely monitor performance, hold the person accountable and provide regular feedback. Be patient in your approach to help them get to where you need them to be.

High Will/High Skill

Here you can delegate, empower and give extra responsibility to the person. This team member needs little hand holding, probably just an initial conversation to set direction. Clarify your expectation and then leave them to get on with the task – with appropriate check-ins and updates.

Low Will/High Skill

Identify the reason for the low will. Tap into what motivates this person by looking at what they value and, where you can, tie that into the task. Provide recognition of their progress to reinforce positive behaviours.

Your job as manager is not to do your team members' jobs. It's to help them understand the bigger picture, develop them and give them space to do their best. So remember, empower don't micromanage.

5. Maintain high levels of performance

People in high-performing teams are good at keeping each other on track and maintaining high levels of performance. They don't let anyone fall behind. These teams are clear on what success looks like and are encouraged to hold each other accountable. Feedback is given in a respectful and timely manner. Think of it as being coached during the game, rather than after the final whistle.

True high-performing teams don't burn themselves out. They take a break at the right time, down tools at the right time and refocus at the right time. The key here is to make sure you're building in enough downtime to maximize your performance. Balance is key.

To maintain high levels of performance, consider the following six elements.

Alignment to the vision, mission and purpose

It is vital that all projects, tasks and assignments are linked to what the organization is trying to achieve. Your team needs to understand how what they do is affecting the success of the organization.

Constant communication

Your people will remain motivated and dedicated to delivering on your goal when they are communicated with often and with the information that they need to know. Include reviews of projects or task progress with any relevant measures.

Positive, high-energy environment

Consider your and your team members' working space if you are able to influence it:

- Natural daylight and possible views
- Chill-out areas – to let off steam or re-energize
- Sound – music?
- Remove distractions – keep your people focused
- Air quality and ventilation
- Design and colour – choose something uplifting and fun
- Temperature – try to find the right balance for everyone.

Celebrate and recognize success

We look at this in more detail in the following section.

Ask for team ideas and innovation

Make sure your team members feel open to suggesting ideas for improvement or innovation, without fear of being made to feel foolish for suggesting it or repercussions for failing. Encouraging this process will breed a culture of trust and mutual respect.

Review achievements or distance travelled

By reviewing achievements or distance travelled, your team will be more aware of where they have fallen short and what they need to do to change course to ensure that the project or task will still be achieved. These reviews can be short term and long term and the feedback is essential to drive improvement.

6. Celebrate and recognize success

Work can feel like a thankless chore if there is no recognition of effort or celebration of achievement. Great managers know this and are brilliant at doing the simple stuff – the 'thank yous' and making sure people receive acknowledgement for their efforts.

Let's return to Ian who kicked off this chapter. He recalls how he and his team discussed issues together before decisions were made. Ian often made presentations to the board and on one occasion he was up just before lunch. He did the presentation and the CEO said it was good and there was much to discuss, but they would do so after lunch. And Ian said, 'Before we break, can I just tell you that 85 per cent of this presentation was produced by Delia who, if you don't know, is an HR manager in the team. And if you were impressed by what you have heard, please comment to her as it will be so motivational.'

As Ian tells it, one of the board directors – a Lord with a major role at a large retailer – came up to him during the buffet lunch and said, 'Why is it that, whenever you do these presentations, you always name people from your team who have contributed?' I said, 'To me, that's perfectly normal. If it's a good presentation and it's gone down well, I would like the person who helped me to be recognized. And if board directors can tell that person it went well, then that means all the more because they wouldn't expect that.'

What's interesting is that this director seemed totally confused by Ian's response. And that is a trap managers can fall into – taking all the glory for themselves. By recognizing the people who contributed, Ian created positive energy and motivation throughout his team and ensured they would want to repeat the success. You can find some recognition techniques in Chapter 2, 'Great goal setting'.

7. Be a role model

You are the role model and your team will take their lead from you. Your actions will be watched way more closely than you can ever imagine and this is the natural pressure that comes with being a leader. As a world-class manager, you have to be aware that you set the tone in terms of your energy and positivity. That's not to say that you can't show vulnerability. In fact, vulnerability is not weak but rather implies you have the courage to be yourself. A survey of 12,000 global employees by Emily Shaffer and Stephanie Neal for Catalyst in 2021 found that people are more willing to go the extra mile at work when their manager shows vulnerability and is open.[5]

World-class managers are skilled at managing their own emotions. They shoulder much responsibility for the atmosphere of the team and should be mindful that every interaction will impact on their people – either positively or negatively. To find out more about role modelling, refer back to Chapter 9 on understanding the customer.

Conclusion

Creating a standout team is a core skill for a world-class manager. It's also one that needs work – especially if you have been promoted into a managerial role from a technical specialist role. You may be the best in the business at operational tasks, but you won't achieve world-class management status unless you bring your team along with you. We will look in more detail at how you can develop that team, by developing yourself, in Chapter 12.

CHECKLIST
Actions to take now

- Write down this checklist and review it on a consistent basis:

  1 Do you have a clear and compelling vision for your team?

  2 Is the team clear about its role in this vision?

  3 Are team members empowered or are you a micromanager?

  4 What's the brand of your team in the business?

  5 How effectively do you promote your team's achievements?

  6 Do your people feel thanked and recognized?

  7 Do you understand how they like to be recognized?

  8 How good is the team at communicating?

- Design or review your ambition for the team. It could be a long-term strategic goal or it could be a short-term project focus. What blocks the team from being high performing? Take some time to think about this. What can be done to remove these blocks?

- Think about someone in your organization whom you would class as high performing. What makes you think that? How can you do the same?

Notes

1 Thangavelu, A and Sudhahar, C (2017) Role Clarity and Job Performance Among the Employees in Small and Medium IT Industries. core.ac.uk/download/pdf/234676026.pdf (archived at perma.cc/96CL-DHA5)

2 Effectory (2019) HR Analytics: Role clarity impacts performance. www.effectory.com/knowledge/hr-analytics-role-clarity-impacts-performance/ (archived at perma.cc/8QA8-UX46)

3 Corporate Rebels (2022) Micromanagement: Corporate Disease No 1. corporate-rebels.com/micromanagement/?mc_cid=514c11578a&mc_eid=c7eeac6b0b (archived at perma.cc/G5PL-YH54)

4 Parker, S, Knight, C and Keller, A (2020) Remote Managers Are Having Trust Issues. hbr.org/2020/07/remote-managers-are-having-trust-issues (archived at perma.cc/W6TZ-32HV)

5 Shaffer, E and Neal, S (2021) Why Leaders Must Connect More During Times of Crisis, Catalyst. www.catalyst.org/research/leaders-connect-during-crisis/ (archived at perma.cc/366N-BC6L)

11
View from the top: Delighting your customer

While working in the Middle East for global banking giant HSBC, Paul Szumilewicz was part of a team that came up with a simple yet effective way of bringing the customer to life in everything they did. It involved hats.

The team mandated that in every meeting someone in the room would represent the customer. To make it more fun and engaging, they kicked off with a conference and put customer hats in all the meeting rooms. In every meeting someone would wear the hat and they then had the responsibility of representing the customer in whatever discussion was taking place.

'It sounds so simple but it was a really impactful tool,' Paul explains. 'It made sure that in everything we did we never forgot what it would mean for the customer. We could be talking about a product or process change or a new supplier we were considering and those with customer hats on would tell us how the customer would respond. What was the customer impact? It's a small example but often the small ideas are the best ones.'

It's a straightforward way of putting yourself in the customer's shoes – a tried and tested approach to understanding your customer so that you can deliver an unrivalled experience. In Paul's experience there are few more powerful ways of delighting the customer than being able to experience, observe and learn from some of the things that they go through in reality.

'For example, I read about a fantastic CEO at Air Asia who, a couple of times a month, blocks out two days and spends time doing the different jobs that people would do within his company, such as putting all the bags onto the conveyor belt. It's a good reminder of how tough some of those jobs are as well as interacting with customers,' he says.

There's one caveat to this approach, however. It's something Paul says he has learnt more about in the past three years – and that is that it is difficult in practice to put yourself in the customer's shoes because customers have different experiences, different backgrounds and different ways of thinking. Instead, managers and their teams need to actively listen to the customer and try to put their own experiences aside, he believes.

> I did just that this week. I sat with some of our customer service teams who take customer calls and I just listened in for an hour to try and get a flavour of what customers call in about. What do they ask? How do they sound? What do they say? What did they get frustrated about? What were they happy about? You do this and you realize it's the most impactful and useful thing you've done all week and you should do it more often. We can all do this – CEOs, senior managers, middle managers, junior managers, all across the board.

Now chief customer officer at the UK's oldest privately owned bank, C Hoare & Co, Paul has oversight and direct responsibility for customer service, customer operations marketing and data science. It's this partnering of people and technology that particularly excites him.

C Hoare at a glance

Banking company C Hoare & Co was founded in 1672 and has been owned continuously by the Hoare family for 12 generations. As such it combines a contemporary bespoke banking service with a conservative attitude to risk which has enabled it to weather three industrial revolutions, the Wall Street Crash and successive global crises. The partners view themselves as stewards of a unique and evolving culture built on personal trust, strong relationships and outstanding customer service, underpinned by the Hoare family values of honesty, empathy, excellence and social responsibility.

His interest was piqued while at HSBC when he was involved in a piece of work they called the 'human advantage'. Out of this work came a core realization, he says. 'In banking in particular, but I suspect many industries would agree, if you believe and agree with anyone who says the future is solely in technology then you've probably already lost. I can't speak for all banks but certainly those I have worked for will not be able to compete with Amazon, Meta, Tencent, Alibaba or whoever when it comes to technology. We'd likely lose the battle.'

Instead, the key is in marrying the best of technology with the best of human. 'Customers require banking experience and knowledge to make the right decisions, to feel secure and to feel like they are being looked after when it comes to their financial needs. So, the research found that it's about the human advantage – the power when both human aspects and technology come together.'

To illustrate this, we can go back to 1997 when world chess champion Garry Kasparov took on IBM supercomputer Deep Blue in a series of chess matches. Deep Blue defeated Kasparov, resulting in these matches being seen as an example of artificial intelligence overtaking humanity. But roll forward to 2005 and chess site Playchess.com staged a freestyle tournament in which anyone could compete in teams with other players or computers. It ended with a shock win by two amateurs defeating teams of grandmasters with state-of-the-art computers. The winners, Steven Cramton and Zackary Stephen, used three computers at the same time and coached them to look deeply into positions. This result prompted Kasparov to write in the *New York Review of Books*: 'Weak human + machine + better process was superior to a strong computer alone and, more remarkably, superior to a strong human +

machine + inferior process.'[1] 'I love that story,' says Paul. 'It shows human creativity, curiosity and communication – the three Cs – are still hard to replicate by computers. So human and computer together can create the types of customer journeys, the types of products and types of services to benefit customers that will be hard to replicate just by humans or just by computers.'

It's perhaps no surprise, then, that Paul believes it's people and their behaviours that are at the heart of delivering a superior customer experience. In fact, he describes himself as a 'talent fanatic, gratitude connoisseur and, at his core, a servant and compassionate leader'.

> Early on in my career, I was fortunate to either be told or learn that if I spent 70–80 per cent of my time focused on my people and making sure that I attracted the right people, retained the right people and made those people feel a million dollars, then the rest would take care of itself. But it takes lots of energy and is not easy.
>
> I love the phrase that great leadership is hard work. It's exhausting, to be honest. But I like to spend a lot of time trying to catch people 'doing things right', explaining what it is that I like and that they did well so they can replicate.

If there were one lesson from Paul that would help a manager become a world-class manager it is to care for your people. 'I wish more managers and leaders were humble and vulnerable and could find their own authentic way to genuinely care about their people.'

In the first week of his new role, he asked his team to tell him what was important to them. Was it their kids? Was it their exercise? Was it looking after someone? Their local church?

> If I help them do what they need to do, what they care about, then guess what? They're much more likely to give me the discretionary effort that no one has to give when they come into work. It's about authenticity in caring. But if you don't naturally do this, it's not easy. You will have to work hard because people will know if you're doing it in a fake way.

And it works the same with customers. If you build that trust, if you build that connection, if you care about your customer, they're much more likely to be loyal and let you off when you do mess up. And they will go to that dinner party and say 'my bank's amazing because I feel they genuinely care for me'. That's how you delight your customers.

TIP

Paul's three tips for being a world-class manager

1. Do one-to-one meetings well

I have lost count of how many managers don't do this. The most important thing in my diary is that always on a Monday I have a weekly check-in with all of my direct reports for half an hour and every Friday I have a weekly checkout. So doing one-to-one meetings well and protecting them in your diary.

2. Be vulnerable

Build trust and be comfortable with being vulnerable. Over the past four or five years I've realized I need to take myself less seriously, reduce my ego and realize that the fact I'm not the smartest person in the room is a good thing. Being able to say, I have no idea what to do either, let's sit down, talk me through it and see if we can figure it out together or if there is anyone else we need to get in. This vulnerability is so powerful for building connection.

3. Give more recognition

Research in *Harvard Business Review* found that in the most effective team environments the ratio of positive feedback to negative was five to one. I reckon I'm somewhere about three to one and that's probably as good as I've seen it. We have a long way to go here because as managers we're generally good at catching people when they've dropped the ball, but how often do we catch people doing things really well and recognize them? It needs to be specific, not just, you are doing a good job but a good job for what? Or I like how you answered that question. So, let's increase how many times we recognize our people.

Notes

1 Kasparov, G (2010) The Chess Master and the Computer. Review of *Chess Metaphors – Artificial Intelligence and the Human Mind*, by Diego Rasskin-Gutman, translated from the Spanish by Deborah Klosky. www.nybooks.com/articles/23592 (archived at perma.cc/ZZY8-CBE9)

12
Developing you, developing your team

Introduction

As a manager, you focus so much on your team and your stakeholders that it can be easy to forget about your own development. But no one is going to care more about your career than you do. Yet only 28.8 per cent of managers we have surveyed say they have a detailed plan to achieve their career goals.

Why does this matter? Well, think about the safety briefing by the cabin crew when you take a flight. One of the main points in the briefing is that you should put on your own oxygen mask before helping someone else with theirs. We're no use to anyone if we're not at our best.

World-class managers understand that the organizations that will win in the future are those that learn the fastest. To thrive in the 21st-century workplace, people therefore need to continue learning. As the Ancient Greek philosopher Heraclitus said, there is nothing permanent except change – and the speed of this change in business is increasing all the time.

Great managers recognize that all situations are potential learning opportunities and that they themselves need to learn continually if they are to lead a great team. A study by leadership advisory firm Egon Zehnder in 2021 found that 78 per cent of CEOs agree that they need to continue their self-transformation – three times more than just three years earlier. They talk about the importance of a 'dual journey' where their own personal development and the organization's growth are interrelated and it is through this that they will get optimal change.[1] As a world-class manager, this inter-relation between your own development and that of your team, and ultimately your business, is similarly important.

One of the main reasons people leave organizations is lack of career growth. I've seen many large multinational companies where people have left for lack of growth reasons. I've also seen many small companies where people have stayed just because they are being grown. McKinsey research involving 13,382 individuals in the United States, UK, Canada, Australia, India and Singapore found that 41 per cent cited the lack of career development and advancement as the reason they left a company between April 2021 and April 2022 – the top reason.[2] So, if you can help your team members develop their skills, as well as ensuring your own are up to date, then this is a major win for your organization.

Indeed, the World Economic Forum puts the ability to under-take 'growth management', that is, the ability to support your peo-ple to grow professionally, as one of the advanced management tasks that cannot be replaced by artificial intelligence in the future, so if you want to remain a world-class manager in the next 10 years, then this focus on growth is one skill you will need to master.[3]

There are several positive effects from taking a more positive stance to planning your career. Your team will be watching how you challenge yourself and will replicate it, especially if you select people who want to continually improve themselves. You are their role model. And you can drive a deeper sense of commitment and of self-worth by demonstrating how the organization is investing in you and your team. The effects on engagement are huge.

The good news from our research is that 70.5 per cent of managers say they are focused on not only developing themselves but their team's career as well. So, there is a recognition that both need to be done. But how to do it? Here are seven steps to develop yourself to develop your team.

The WCM 7

- Take ownership of your career.
- Take stock of where you currently are.
- Create a vision and exciting goals for yourself.
- Develop a plan to execute that vision.
- Develop a personal brand.
- Find a mentor or sponsor.
- Help your team to develop their careers.

1. Take ownership of your career

A common plea we hear from CEOs, senior leaders and HR directors is 'Please tell our people to take ownership of their careers. Tell them to not sit and wait for things to come their way but to go out there, be proactive and drive their own careers.'

Think of it like this. If you were the CEO of your own career, how might that change the way you think and what you do?

Before you prepare for the future, it's important that you understand what traits and behaviours got you to where you are now, for both yourself and your team members:

- Reflect on your strengths, weaknesses, areas for development, fears, values and personal brand (how you are perceived by others).

- Visualize your career future and that of your team members. Take time to speak with your people to ask them who and what they want to be in the future. They will need to think about where the sector is going, what changes might be on the horizon and to identify if there are any future opportunities for them.

They could think about what experience or skills might be required in the future. They could also visualize where they want to be in three to five years' time and pre-write their CV, imagining the job description and identifying what they would need to have done in their job roles to prepare for that job.

2. Take stock of where you currently are

Ask yourself some of the questions below:

- Where am I now and am I 100 per cent satisfied?
- If everything worked out the way I wanted it to, where would I like to be and in what timeframe?
- Where are the opportunities for me?
- How can I get there and who can help me?

1 *Do this regularly*

Put it in your diary to take stock regularly, weekly, monthly or yearly. You need to schedule for it and make sure you remove any distractions from the review session.

2 *Highlight your achievements*

It is really beneficial for you to write down what you have achieved to date. Keeping a record of your achievements, big and small, will help you realize what you are capable of. It will also be really useful if you are planning a career change and need to update your CV.

3 *Review your sector*

Whichever industry or sector you work in, it is crucial to keep abreast of sector trends and innovation. This will not only benefit you in your current role but also prepare you for the future and what it could mean for your career.

4 *Transferable skills*

While taking stock, you should also identify what transferable skills you may have gained in your current role. This could include skills in areas such as IT, accounting, interviewing, time management, sales, customer service, budgeting, etc.

3. Create a vision and exciting goals for yourself.

If you were to imagine an exciting future, what would it look like? And if everything went according to plan, where would you like to be in 12, 24, 36 months' time?

Take some time to think about what would energize you and excite you. Research shows us that the brain responds positively to clear goals that excite and focus us. So get those creative juices flowing.

As we saw in Chapter 2, organizations set visions and goals, so take these same principles and apply them to yourself. Great goals can create real energy and focus and really help you achieve your ambitions.

4. Develop a plan

Once you are clear about your vision, how can you make it happen? And who can help you? Your manager is a good first port of call but you can also look for a sponsor or mentor (see point 6 below). Look at what additional competencies you may need and what additional duties could help you bridge the gap between the job role you have now and where you want to get to.

Check out any extra teams you can get involved in to develop your skills. Your organization may have task forces or project teams. Or you could volunteer for public-speaking opportunities. Activities such as these will increase your visibility in the organization and help you to be considered for that next step.

Apply the SMART goal-setting principles from Chapter 2 to develop your plan. Make sure you have regular one-to-ones with your manager to review progress and get their support.

5. Develop a personal brand

I could write a whole book on this and indeed there are many excellent books out there on how to develop your personal brand. But I think a quote from Amazon-founder Jeff Bezos neatly sums this point up when he says, 'Your brand is what people say about you when you are not in the room.'

Do you know what they are saying about you? Our research with 589 global managers found that nearly half (49.6 per cent) say they are not clear on how they are perceived by their team members and only 42 per cent say they actively manage their personal brand.

World-class managers and executives I've met all over the world actively manage their personal brand. It's an important part of career management. I recommend all managers do the same. Here's what you can do:

1 Actively manage your stakeholders and network. Do you have good relationships with people who could matter to your career and advancement? Do you invest time in coffees and lunches with key stakeholders? Find out about them and let them know more about you and what you are doing.

2 Actively manage your interactions. A mantra of one successful manager we worked with was 'every interaction is an opportunity to enhance or diminish your brand'. Their attitude was: make sure you make every single interaction count.

3 Understand the expectations of your key stakeholders and make sure that you meet them.

4 Find out what's important to them and make sure your activity, your behaviour and your communication are completely aligned with those expectations.

5 Put time in your calendar every week to review how your brand management is going. Find just 20 minutes to reflect on what you have done for your personal brand and any feedback you have had.

6 Look for opportunities to build profile and exposure either within your business or externally. Get involved in different kinds of projects or think about public-speaking opportunities.

Be clear on how you want and need to be perceived. What qualities do you have that you would like people to associate with you and what unique skills and attributes do you possess that can distinguish you and make you stand out from the crowd? All of these are part of developing and thinking about how you can push your brand forward.

6. Find a mentor or sponsor

Having an influential ally can really help you to progress towards your goal. They can also help you understand and navigate some of the politics in the organization and the unwritten rules about how people can progress. A good sponsor can also advocate on your behalf.

In her 2013 book *Forget a Mentor, Find a Sponsor: The new way to fast-track your career*, economist Sylvia Ann Hewlett found that male employees with a sponsor are 23 per cent more likely to get that next promotion than those who do not have a sponsor. For women the figure was 19 per cent.[4]

So, getting a sponsor, or mentor, is a proven way of improving your career. Consider these four points before selecting one.

Think what kind of mentor you want/need

Think about your situation and where you are in your career. Review your career goals – short term and long term. Then think about how your potential mentor's skills and experience could help you achieve these goals.

Make a list

Once you have thought about the kind of mentor that you want or need, you can start to list any potential individuals who would be a good fit. Think about anyone whom you look up to and who has achieved the types of things you are looking to emulate. They may have achieved accolades within your company or sector or be in a future position that you would like to be in.

Review your network

It is best to start by reviewing your existing network, as it makes more sense to ask someone whom you know or have an existing relationship with.

Explain your choice

Once you have selected your potential mentor, you will need to clearly explain to them why you feel that you need them and what you want to get out of the relationship. Take time to review their history and background to show that you have given it some thought and explain why their experience and skill set would be valuable to you if they agreed to be your mentor.

7. Help your team to develop their careers

Showing people that you care about their development is a huge motivator and great managers are very aware of this. Consider how you can be a great coach and mentor to your own team members and help them to grow and achieve their potential. As we see from Sylvia Ann Hewett's research, being a protégé of a mentor or sponsor is great for your career. But did you know that sponsoring someone else as a manager is also of great benefit to your career?

In Hewett's recent book *The Sponsor Effect: How to be a better leader by investing in others*, she reveals new research that found middle-level managers who have protégés are 167 per cent more likely to be given stretch assignments and senior executives who sponsor rising talent are 53 per cent more likely to be promoteds.

Conclusion

As a manager, you spend much of your time focusing on day-to-day activities, directing what is happening in the present rather than thinking about the future. But as we have seen in this chapter, by carefully considering where you want to go and what you want to be known for, you will reap the benefits for yourself, your team and your organization. It's important you carve out some time to take a deep delve into this. As we will see in the next chapter, taking ownership of your own career and those of your team members will help you to be viewed positively by your own manager.

CHECKLIST
Actions to take now

- Review your stakeholder mapping from Chapter 1 and carry out a brand audit. Seek feedback on how you are perceived by your key stakeholders.

- Create a plan of action to develop your relationships and personal brand. Identify who can help you.

- Reflect on how you are developing your team. Are you clear on what their dreams and ambitions are? On what their development and opportunity areas are? Consider how you can help them get there.

Notes

1 Egon Zehnder (2021) CEO Study. www.egonzehnder.com/it-starts-with-the-CEO (archived at perma.cc/7MZW-5UZC)
2 McKinsey (2022) Great Attrition, Great Attraction 2.0 Global Survey [Accessed 31 August 2022]

3 World Economic Forum (2020) These 6 Skills Cannot Be Replicated by Artificial Intelligence. www.weforum.org/agenda/2020/10/these-6-skills-cannot-be-replicated-by-artificial-intelligence/ (archived at perma.cc/3PD9-QQMQ)

4 Sylvia Ann Hewlett, S A (2013) *Forget a Mentor, Find a Sponsor: The new way to fast-track your career*. Harvard Business Review Press, Cambridge, MA

5 Hewlett, S A (2019) *The Sponsor Effect: How to be a better leader by investing in others*. Harvard Business Review Press, Cambridge, MA

13

Be skilful at managing up

Introduction

It's coming to the end of the month. You are still way off your revenue target and there are only a few days to go. Your boss is breathing down your neck. This is a vital month for the business. As a world-class manager, you bring your team together, brainstorm some new ideas and develop an action plan to get to that target. You put in extra hours, encourage your team by recognizing the great work they are doing, and you role model by approaching potential customers yourself. And then you do it. At the 11th hour you pull in a big new customer and not only hit but go way over the target. Not only that, but this customer is a perfect fit for the organization and there is plenty more business that can come from them. And you know you can deliver a great service to them. It's the proverbial win-win.

And then? In a perfect world your boss comes rushing over, congratulates the team, recognizes the effort and contribution you have personally made and maybe even opens a bottle of champagne. The next day your manager's boss pops their head in the door and thanks you and the team. You can see that bonus getting nearer. Maybe even a promotion. Certainly a contender for team of the year.

Instead, you get nothing. Not even a verbal thank you. No mention in dispatches. Worst still, you hear that your boss has been taking all the glory at board level.

This is a common story. It may not be about revenue but perhaps hitting a marketing target or meeting a deadline for a complex project. Whatever it is, many of us have been in the position where we have gone above and beyond only to be ignored by our own manager and to see them patted on the back for our work. But, of course, had we not hit that target then we would at best have been pulled in to explain ourselves and at worst incurred the wrath of our manager.

Why does this matter? After all, there is an argument that by letting your boss bask in the glory you are helping them to look successful and that will benefit you in the longer term. However, as we discovered earlier in the book, many people leave their jobs because of their manager – and you are no different.

Your relationship with your boss is one of the most crucial you will have and, as such, understanding how to 'manage up' is critical if you are to be successful. I use the terminology of 'managing up' here to mean the person who is more senior to you in your organization by grade or by band. This person has a big effect, not only on how we feel coming to work day to day but on the operation of our teams, on our goals, on our objectives and on our ability to serve the customer, either internally or externally. Their behaviour with their peers also has an effect on how others see you and your team. Ideally, we want our managers to be ambassadors for us and our teams.

Being able to manage up effectively is a challenge for managers, especially those at the start of their managerial career. But creating a positive relationship with all your peers is critical, as we need them to get things done. Effectively you are selling yourself to your boss in terms of your ability to get stuff done for them and for them to trust you. However, it is a balancing act. Chris Roebuck, a global leadership speaker who was appointed honorary visiting professor of transformational leadership at Bayes Business School in 2009, notes the danger of spending all your time trying to impress your boss. 'It's about taking a 360 approach. We've all seen people who fall into the trap of trying to please their boss above all else while effectively crucifying their team. If you focus just on keeping the boss happy, you won't have a team at the end of it – and then your boss is certainly not going to be happy.'

You should be aiming to build an open, honest, effective working relationship. Imagine for a moment that your boss is a customer. When we look at the customer, we're looking at someone from the perspective of understanding their needs, what is it they want, how can we delight them, what's their challenge and why. The same applies to those more senior than us. Find out what are their challenges, their objectives and what their own boss wants from them. Once you've got a handle on these you stand a chance of delivering for them. It's about making sure you are on the same page as them.

Unfortunately, you may sometimes get a boss whose only interest is in maximizing performance, which optimizes their own career development. If you build up an accurate analysis of why your boss is doing what they are doing and you come to the conclusion they essentially don't care about you or the team, just themselves, then you as a manager can to some degree protect your team from the boss. You may be able to manage your work with little interaction with your manager. But in the worst-case scenario this may start to degrade your own performance over time because it puts you under significant stress and at that stage the best choice may be to leave.

Chris Roebuck recounts a story illustrating just this from his time at a global bank. A long-term Swiss manager retired and an American manager was catapulted in to lead the Zurich-based team. He explains:

> Within three months you could see the atmosphere in the office. People were feeling crushed. This guy had been moved to Switzerland as part of his career development to show that he was good everywhere in the world. So, his one objective was to maximize performance at whatever the cost. But he didn't understand the

culture in Switzerland, the fact that even if someone were five levels below board level they were treated as part of the family. Also, due to Swiss national service, there was a good chance senior leaders had served in the army with other leaders. In the end it was through this network that the American was basically told to behave himself, or he would be back on a plane to America.

In this case, others stepped in to prevent team members leaving. World-class managers can head this off earlier by seeing how to turn a difficult relationship around. I suggest you start with stakeholder management, as outlined in Chapter 1. Remember, managing up has nothing to do with how well you do your job, how much other people may like you or how much the customer may love you. It has everything to do with your personal relationship with your boss. If you can get this right, it's great for your career, as you will be seen as a more valuable asset. But the pitfall here is to not get pigeonholed because you just make someone's life easier. Be careful with this one.

Our research found that 73.1 per cent of managers say they understand the needs of their manager, while 82.3 per cent say they are open and honest with their boss. World-class managers act as partners with the people who manage them. It's an adult-to-adult relationship. The outcome of successfully managing up will be to begin to work in a partnership-like way, where both parties feel their objectives/needs are being met. Here's how to do this.

The WCM 7

- Help your manager to be successful.
- Be clear on your manager's expectations and ensure you are 100 per cent aligned.
- Show empathy for your manager.
- Have a can-do attitude.

- Be proactive and take ownership.
- Bring ideas to the table.
- Give your manager feedback.

1. Help your manager to be successful

This is one of the golden rules of managing up – it will ensure you are seen as a valuable asset in your manager's eyes. So, spend some time thinking about how your manager is judged and measured by their manager. How can you support them and make them look good in the eyes of their boss?

Attention to detail

Think of the old saying 'measure twice, cut once'. This motto is applicable in any work-related situation. It is vital you get things done on time, but to ensure that you and your manager are perceived in the right way, your quality and precision must be first class too – especially when you're working on a project, proposal or presentation for your manager. Whenever possible, try to slow down and re-read a message or email before you send it, or re-read a proposal to ensure you are sending the best possible version. Or ask a colleague to check your work before you are too hasty in submitting your project or idea.

Keep your manager up to speed

Keep your manager in the loop on the important matters – and sometimes the not so important. If your manager is asked about an issue or incident that they do not know about ahead of time, it makes it seem like they do not know what is happening in their team. If they look bad to their own manager, this will reflect on you too. Even if the matter seems trivial, if there are possible repercussions you must inform your manager. This will build trust between you and will enable you to find ways to prevent any further issues in the future.

Latest trends

Wherever possible, you should try to stay abreast of the latest trends in your sector. In doing so you could find new technologies, sales techniques or marketing trends that could benefit your department or organization as a whole. Share what you have found with your manager, then they can amplify your findings. They will look good and so will you.

Find solutions

If you are constantly going to your manager with problems and not considering what the possible solutions could be beforehand, you will be adding to your manager's workload and giving them more stress. By considering all situations and finding some possible solutions, you will have already removed the time-consuming concern your manager will feel. This shows a maturity in your approach and will help your manager to proceed with full knowledge and possible options for dealing with problems.

2. Be clear on your manager's expectations and ensure you are 100 per cent aligned

What does your manager need from you in terms of performance or communication and behaviour? What does good look like in their eyes? Are you clear on this? I see so many great people get this wrong because they are not 100 per cent clear on their manager's expectations.

If you're not clear, find out. It is not only an opportunity for you to have a meaningful conversation with them, but it will show you care about giving them what they need.

What is your manager's style?

You can start by closely observing your manager and learning everything you can about their management style. Are they someone who likes quick responses, do they prefer to consider ideas thoroughly before making a decision, are they focused on the financial impact or do they have high standards? Do they want all the facts and figures or do they like a little humour? Try to consider all their management traits and incorporate these into how you interact with your manager.

Get to know your manager

If possible, get to know your manager on a work level and a personal level. Find out what challenges they may be facing or personal issues they may have. It will help both of you when trying to collaboratively achieve something as a team.

Have regular meetings

Our research found that two-thirds of managers often check in with their manager to show they are on the same page. It is important to check in with your manager regularly, even if it's only 20 minutes a week. This time should be scheduled in, and you can cover items such as completed projects or successes, any ongoing projects or tasks and finally any future projects or items to be discussed. You can also use this time to keep your manager up to date with any problems or issues that may need resolving.

Become an expert

Try to gain as much knowledge and skills as possible in your current role. This way you will become the go-to person for assistance and guidance. Your manager will value the experience and help that you have been providing.

3. Show empathy for your manager

Being a manager can be tough sometimes, as you will know, so put yourself in your manager's shoes. What does the world look like through their eyes? What are their pressures, their wants and worries? What keeps them up at night? What is their personal style and preference?

Think about what a typical day looks like for your manager. It would be good to find out what their frustrations or difficult parts of their role are, so that you could find ways to eliminate some of them and in turn make their life better. By finding out what is important to them, you can work with them to achieve a common goal.

One of the best ways to get to know your manager is to ask them questions when you meet with them. Consider the following questions:

- What are your goals?
- What frustrates you?
- What would help you do your job better or more easily?
- What pressures are you under?
- What do you expect from me?

Thinking through these questions will help you better align with your manager.

4. Have a can-do attitude

Managers need people they can count on, so you need to build trust and have a positive can-do attitude. But be mindful: 'can do' can be a double-edged sword. If you have too much on, you may need to say no sometimes.

Growth mindset

The concept of a growth versus fixed mindset was coined by Carol Dweck, a Stanford University psychologist. A fixed mindset means you believe you have unchanging traits. Those characteristics dictate what you think you can do. Thinking of yourself as unintelligent is an example of a fixed mindset. A growth mindset is about believing in the effects of the experience and learning that have got you where you are today. People with a growth mindset are more resilient to stress and negative situations or outcomes. They believe that anything can be overcome and achieved when the right effort and consideration are put into them.

Positive mental attitude

We've all had that nagging voice in our heads telling us to do something different. For many, that voice is their harshest critic. For those with a can-do attitude, they will hear themselves saying things like 'come on, we've got this'. Thinking positively includes speaking positively to yourself. Try to avoid saying 'I can't do this' or 'It's never going to work'. Instead, try to think about how you can work around issues or bumps in the road and keep the language positive. You've got this!

Learn from your mistakes

We all make mistakes and, although painful at the time, they can be a positive way of learning and growing from the experience. Once you have accepted responsibility for the error, try to reflect on why it happened, what could be done differently and how you can put measures in place to stop it happening again. Then move on from it.

5. Be proactive and take ownership

Your manager is not a mind reader and is probably juggling many challenging priorities. If you do need something, let them know. Don't wait for them to come to you or complain that they are not giving it to you.

How to be more proactive

1 Don't wait for feedback. Actively seek it from your manager. This shows a willingness to learn and improve.
2 Be proactive in sharing feedback. Wherever possible, share your thoughts, suggestions, ideas and feedback.

3 Don't be afraid to ask questions. This way you will be equipped with the knowledge and information that you need to do your job well and you will also be seen as being proactive in your role.

How to be less reactive

1 *Planning.* Always try to plan ahead and consider what might come up before it happens. Proactive people spend time thinking ahead so they are prepared for all eventualities.

2 *Prioritize:* Proactive people review any problems or issues and set priorities on each, rather than worrying about what they should do in the moment. Take some time to review any issues and how they can be resolved well ahead of time.

3 *Positive language:* Try to consider the words you use, as it will have an effect on those around you. If you say things like 'I have to do this' or 'If I only had the time, I would', it creates a negative feeling. Try to use phrases like 'I am going to do this' or 'I will do that'.

6. Bring ideas to the table

No one has the monopoly on good ideas and if you can come up with good suggestions, bring new improved ideas for processes, performance, strategy or delivery, it will help your manager and enhance their perception of your value. I often hear senior leadership talk glowingly about people who do this well. Work out what your manager's main motivation is, and you can match your idea to it.

1 *Highlight the benefits of your idea:* Show them how the idea would help them, the team and the business as a whole.

2 *Present your main/best idea first:* Write down all your ideas and prioritize what is most important; that idea should be presented first. You can touch on the other areas of your idea during your pitch but keep a focus on the main idea.

3 *Give options:* It is good to have some backup options to present if your original proposition isn't quite hitting the mark. It will show that you have considered everything in detail and all options available.

4 *Ask for feedback:* You need to practise how to respond to potential questions your manager may have. Perhaps present your idea to some of your colleagues first and get them to think about possible questions, and then consider how you might answer them.

5 *Give credit to others:* If you asked for help from your colleagues and peers then you need to ensure that they are given the right credit. Your manager needs to know who should be recognized for their efforts.

6 *Have a plan:* You must have a plan for how you are going to implement any suggested ideas, including a step-by-step plan of how it will work.

7. Give your manager feedback

Feedback is a gift, so do be open when your manager gives you feedback. Try to hear it in a positive light and if it is developmental, try not to take it personally. If you feel your manager is micromanaging, it may be that they feel you have behaviours that hinder your performance. Be open to their feedback as you may not realize your own blind spots.

But equally, have the courage to share your feedback. No one is perfect and there may be things your manager does that they are not aware of that you can help them with. The rule of thumb is always to be respectful and to give the feedback with empathy, so that it doesn't feel judgemental or personal.

Our research found that just over three-quarters (76.7 per cent) of managers would not hesitate to share feedback and concerns with their manager. Therefore, one in four are not comfortable doing this. It can be hard to give feedback to someone above you. So, make it about the issues or the good of the enterprise to take the personal element out of it. Remember, feedback should always be delivered with a positive intent.

Conclusion

Managing up can be tricky, so it is useful to think about your manager as a customer. In this scenario you are providing a service to your manager. What do they want from you? How do they want to use your skills? How do they like getting information from you? If you view it like this, you can manage their expectations.

An added complication today is the move to hybrid and remote work in some organizations. In such situations, ensuring your contribution is 'seen' is all the more important, especially if you do not work traditional hours. Develop a consistent way of communicating regularly with your boss to demonstrate the work you have done. Go on the offensive here rather than waiting for your boss to ask you.

By managing your boss effectively, you develop a two-way relationship based on mutual respect, co-operation and understanding. They rely on you to be honest, reliable and to deliver value. You rely on them to set priorities, get your critical resources and link you to the rest of the organization. Together you will have a healthy relationship that enables you both to thrive.

CHECKLIST
Actions to take now

- Get clarity on your manager's perception of your impact. Are you giving them what they need and helping them be successful? Ask yourself what opportunities there are to enhance your impact with them and plan how you will achieve this.

- Modify your communication style to make your conversations with your manager more effective. Understand how they best want to communicate and adapt your behaviour accordingly. If they like short catch-ups, ensure you have all the information you need ready to deliver concisely. If they like emails, consider the best way to express yourself clearly in this medium.

- Review how open and honest your conversations with your manager are. Ask yourself what's working well. Is there a conversation you could have to enhance your relationship with them?

14
Presenting with presence

Introduction

The comedian Jerry Seinfeld once said, 'I guess we'd rather be in the casket than delivering the eulogy.' He was referring to the fear of public speaking many of us have, and if you are one of them, you're not alone. A survey we conducted with 544 managers found that 45 per cent of them said they did not have confidence when presenting.

The often-quoted 1973 American Fears study by RH Bruskin Associates of 3,000 US inhabitants which examined people's biggest fears revealed that death came in at number 7 and public speaking at number 1. A 2012 study carried out to verify these results confirmed that public speaking was selected more often than any other as a common fear, though when participants were asked to select a top fear death unsurprisingly came top.[1]

So, why do so many people find public speaking daunting or even scary? It's rooted in psychology and all about the fear of being rejected. No one wants to be rejected. In fact, the fear we often experience is because we feel out of control. You know the feeling: heart racing, clammy hands, shallow breathing. But there is so much we can take control of, which we will explore.

Chris Anderson, curator of the popular TED Talks series, notes that presentations rise or fall on the quality of the idea, the narrative and the passion of the speaker. 'It's about substance, not speaking style or multimedia pyrotechnics. If you have something to say, you can build a great talk,' he says.[2]

Think of presentations that have wowed you – and those that haven't. I bet those in the former category came from someone energetic, passionate, with lots of eye contact and a good story to tell.

Not only is removing the fear of speaking desirable in itself, being good at presenting in public is important for our 'brand'. In most organizations, being a good public presenter or speaker is valued, both by the organization and by your team, as it impacts on how well we can communicate so many of the key messages we've talked about in other chapters.

A key part of presenting well is holding people's attention or having presence. In our survey, 48.3 per cent of managers felt that they could hold people's attention while presenting. Presenting with presence is just that – it's about having presence so that who you are and what you say is memorable and drives people to act. It is a key foundation to being a world-class manager.

The WCM 7

- Take control of **how** you present.
- Know your audience.
- Determine what the purpose of your presentation is.
- Decide what your main point is.
- Create the presentation structure.
- Bring your points to life.
- Practise, practise, practise.

1. Take control of how you present

Albert Mehrabian's famous 7-38-55 communication model says that only 7 per cent of our first impression is due to the content of what we are saying, while 55 per cent is due to body language and 38 per cent is due to our voice.[3] He's not saying that content is only 7 per cent important but it is how that content is delivered that makes all the difference. Having said that, before you can present you have to have something to present.

There is a magic ingredient that will drive your presentation and it is what we call our communication energy. Now, that is not about being falsely 'energetic' like some over-excited chat show host, that would be ridiculous, but it is about having a genuine commitment to your message and to your audience and making that intent visible in your delivery.

On a scale of 0–100, we would say that we need to be at 75 per cent+ on energy to really look and sound like you care about what you are saying. So many speakers we see communicate with too low a level of energy and it really doesn't do them or their message justice. One of our key responsibilities as a communicator is to energize our audience.

But energy is not a fake extra that we spray on top; it comes from a genuine conviction and belief in what we are saying, a real emotional engagement with our topic. If we want to have genuine energy, we need to be authentic, otherwise it sounds and looks fake, and authenticity is a key part of communication presence.

That energy should be visible in our body language and audible in our voices. Simply put, low energy = low engagement. How many presenters do you see who have low communication energy? What is the impact of that on the audience? Is it really engaging? Now think about your own energy level and what level you normally communicate at, not only in formal presentations but also generally in meetings. Is it in that 75 per cent + zone?

As well as delivering your presentation energetically, here are some additional tips for getting your audience's attention and keeping it.

- Make good, focused eye contact and share it around the room. In our recent survey of 544 managers, eye contact was one of the two top things they felt they were poor at during presentations.

- The second highlighted issue from the survey was the use of gestures and body language. Use your hands and arms to help you describe and emphasize your messages. Closed body language, such as having your hands behind your back, folded, rigidly clasped together or in your pockets, can all communicate defensiveness or a too casual approach. Many managers feel they suffer from a weak use of gestures, so work to develop your skills in this area or you may look uncommitted during your presentation.

- Make sure you stand in a good, grounded way, with weight on both feet. If you are sitting, sit upright in the chair in a way that communicates that you are engaged and care. Bad posture – standing or sitting – can often be misread as lack of engagement or confidence.

- Avoid fidgeting or shuffling around. We call this 'leaky energy', and it occurs when we are either uncomfortable or not committing enough. A good tip here is to 'get grounded' on your feet and put your energy into your voice and gestures at that 75+ energy level.

- Use the entire range of your voice. The human voice is an incredible instrument that is such an important asset to good communicators. It has incredible potential for expression and variety and yet most communicators use only a small part of it. Think of your voice like a piano with the full range of 88 keys.

- Talk to, and not at, your audience. Or to put it another way, dialogue, not download. People who 'talk at' audiences are very hard to listen to for any length of time. An energized, conversational tone is far more engaging than someone who is just talking at you. 'Make dialogue, not download' should be one of your mantras.

- Vary the tone of your delivery. Audiences love variety in a speaker's delivery, and it helps them engage. Vary it so that it relates to your topic and to how you want the audience to feel. If you want them to feel excited, you need to look and sound excited, otherwise your audience may not be. A monotone delivery is deadly and if your tone stays the same, even if you're talking about different topics, it can seem that you're not fully emotionally engaged or committed to your topic.

- Speak up. If you speak too quietly you might sound unconfident or uncommitted. You need that 75 per cent+ energy in your voice.

- Speed kills. Speaking too quickly is a common mistake, especially if you're nervous or anxious. When you practise your speech beforehand, try to get down to around 110 words per minute. If you go too fast, you don't give people enough time to process your messages and they can very quickly disengage as a result. It is like the tennis practice machines which throw out the balls from one end of the court. Get the pace right and you can have a brilliant practice session – too fast and you'll get frustrated and potentially stop wanting to play.

- Use pauses in your delivery and give yourself permission to pause. Pausing is important to give your listeners time to think and process your messages and creates a real feeling of dialogue. It also gives you time to think so you don't feel the need to keep going without proper time to compose your thoughts. Our mantra as speakers should always be stop–think–speak. Using pauses well can also make you appear more confident and give you an air of gravitas. Pausing also gives you time to read the room, to check in with people and take a breath.

2. Know your audience

Knowing you're going to give your audience something that will keep them interested and engaged is part of the battle of building your confidence ahead of a presentation. But before you get into the details of the content itself, watch some presentations online, find a style that you like and adapt it to create your own style which you think will work for your audience. Getting a clear idea of the personality style of your audience will help you tailor your presentation to their needs.

To help you determine their style, ask yourself these key questions:

- What does your audience need from you in terms of content and style?
- What is their personality and their communication preferences?
- Do they like presentations to be short and sharp with a few key facts and bullet points? Or do they like lots of detail?
- Do they like presentations with a story, emotion and feeling?
- Do they prefer big picture thinking with a few facts presented in the most engaging and dynamic way possible?

3. Determine what the purpose of your presentation is

After weighing up your potential audience by answering the questions above, consider these points regarding the structure of the content itself:

- Why am I speaking?
- What is the desired outcome I want to achieve?
- What do my audience need to think and feel for me to achieve that?

4. Decide what your main point is

What is your key point? It is amazing how many presentations we've watched where this is not clear. Try to distil things down and stay focused. If you only had a minute or two to get your point over, what would you say?

Imagine you had only 30 seconds in the lift with your boss to sell them your idea for the presentation. Come up with an 'elevator pitch' and a key headline and takeaways your audience will remember. This will help focus your messaging.

5. Create the presentation structure

Create a beginning with a message and tone to hook people and set the scene effectively. Your introduction is the first thing people hear and see, so start strongly. Then make sure you create a strong ending and finale to bring the presentation to a strong close. The last thing you want to do is fizzle out at the end, as it will be the last thing people remember.

When developing a strong narrative between the beginning and end, it is useful to think about no more than three points. This Rule of 3 is a classic which will to help to focus your messaging.

6. Bring your points to life

So now you have your structure, think about how you can bring those points to life to engage both your audience's hearts and their minds. Here are some tips to do that:

- Instead of just delivering linear lists of facts, try to use those facts to tell a story. Storytelling is an incredibly powerful way to get messages across and it is the way we create meaning and make sense of the world. A great question to ask yourself is, what's the best story to tell here? Share stories and examples with your audience. Using relevant stories from your experience is a great way to engage people as they allow them to 'see' what you are describing much more clearly. For example, you could highlight some of the great work you have done and the impact that it has made, on the business, your customers or your team. Analogies, metaphors, quotes and examples from external contexts are also a great way to add colour.

- Personalize the content so that you share your point of view, as this is a powerful way of engaging your audience. Use 'I' statements to give the audience a sense of who you are and what you stand for. But also recognize when to use 'we' – when you're referring to an experience or viewpoint.

- Choose your words carefully. Beware of using too much jargon and too many acronyms unless all of the audience really understand them. Speaking in the audience's 'language' is important for connection.

7. Practise, practise, practise

Once you have prepared your presentation the golden rule is practise, practise, practise. No professional actor would go on stage without rehearsal, and no presenter should present without having gone through their material out loud at least three times. Rehearsal will help you to get a sense of flow, where to emphasize, where you need to adjust, edit or add material. I recommend you do this for every presentation.

8. The extra eighth – visual materials

Only after you are clear on points 1 to 6 should you think about the visual support you need. When it comes to slides, less really is more. Try to keep your slides to a minimum and make them visual as much as possible, keeping the text on them to a minimum, with not too many points. Highlight your key points in succinct phrases. Audiences can't listen to you and read detailed, text-heavy slides at the same time.

Conclusion

Presenting can and should be a positive experience. This is a chance to experiment with your style and get feedback afterwards.

Feedback is a great way to learn, yet only 27.6 per cent of managers we surveyed always ask for feedback after presenting. Great presenters continually improve their approach and know that a presentation is an opportunity for personal PR. Do it well and you will enhance your reputation and your executive presence, preparing you well for the next step into strategic leadership, which we discuss in the next chapter.

CHECKLIST
Actions to take now

- Review one of your recent presentations. If you had applied some of the ideas in this chapter, what difference would they have made to your approach? Think about a forthcoming presentation and consider which new ideas you might want to apply to it – in terms of both content and delivery.

- Seek feedback on your presentation impact and general communication ability. Create an evaluation process and a plan for enhancement.

- Think about how you can showcase your work and your capability better by using some of the ideas in this chapter.

Notes

1 Dwyer, K and Davidson, M (2012) Is Public Speaking Really More Feared Than Death? *Communication Research Reports*, 29(2), 99–107. DOI: 10.1080/08824096.2012.667772

2 Anderson, C (2013) How to Give a Killer Presentation. hbr.org/2013/06/how-to-give-a-killer-presentation (archived at perma.cc/XZT5-TYDD)

3 Mehrabian's 7-38-55 Communication Model: It's More Than Words. worldofwork.io/2019/07/mehrabians-7-38-55-communication-model/ (archived at perma.cc/E64U-FLUG)

15
View from the top: World-class management in a family business

Never work with children or animals, said American comedian WC Fields when referring to show business. You could add 'never work with family' to this statement. For while philosopher and poet George Santayana may have declared 'the family is one of nature's masterpieces', we all know that families can be a place of intrigue, strife and dysfunction. Consider those TV families we love to hate: the Ewings in *Dallas*, the Lyons in *Empire*, the Lannisters in *Game of Thrones* or the eponymous Sopranos to name just a few.

And yet families own and manage the majority of businesses worldwide, according to the first *2019/2020 Global Entrepreneurship Monitor Family Entrepreneurship Report* produced by Babson College. Three-quarters of entrepreneurs and 81 per cent of established business owners co-own and/or co-manage their business with family members. In the UK family businesses represent 86.2 per cent of private sector businesses and generated 44.3 per cent of all turnover in the private sector in 2019, found *The State of the Nation: The UK Family Business Sector 2020–2021* report from the IFB Research Foundation and Oxford Economics.

While many of these family businesses are microbusinesses or sole traders, some of the most successful companies in the world are still majority owned by family members (think US retail giant Walmart or German supermarket chain Aldi, Indian multinational conglomerate Tata or luxury goods empire LVMH). So, as a manager you could well find yourself working in a family organization at some time in your career.

How does working in a family business differ from being employed in other types of corporation? Who better to ask than Rupa Patel, executive director at Day Lewis Group, one of the UK's and Europe's largest community pharmacy businesses, and a passionate advocate for family businesses – and world-class management:

> People often think family businesses can have quite a narrow focus but, in reality, most family businesses are great at harnessing the capabilities of their employees as well as their family members. So, for me, when you talk about family values, that's not just around family members but about everybody buying into our values. We see our colleagues as part of the family.
>
> We also have the advantage of being able to have long-term thinking and stability. All the family businesses I speak to have that same mentality. You don't make a short-term decision today that will impact your business for the future. So much of what we talk about is growth, because if you grow, it gives your people more opportunities. But we also talk about being secure and how we can pass on something bigger and better to the next generation than we took on. We're passionate about being able to give back to our colleagues, so it's about how we create an environment that they really want to work in, feel like they can contribute towards and in which they also feel valued as well. Our managers are absolutely vital in that.

Day Lewis Group at a glance

The Day Lewis Group was founded in 1975 by the late Kirit Patel and his brother JC Patel when they opened one pharmacy in Southborough, Kent. It is now led by siblings Jay, Rupa and Sam and has 270 pharmacies across the UK, making it one of the largest independent and long-standing community pharmacy businesses in the UK and Europe. The company employs 2,600 people, of whom only 200 are in a support function; the rest are on the frontline or in warehouses supplying more than 4,000 pharmaceutical products to its retail estate. It also has the pharmacy concession in world-famous department store Harrods in London.

Rupa says she loves the 'passion, people and values' of being in the family business. It helps that she runs a business that has such a strong purpose: 'To help people in the community and feel better.'

> Everybody in the business saves lives every single day, regardless of where they work in our business. I often remind people of that because, at the end of the day, we are looking after families and looking after very sick patients. When they're ill and you can deliver the medication to them and you can see that they're getting better, it feels great. This purpose-driven aspect is really important to the business and our colleagues.

The company purpose is underpinned by core values, including keeping the caring, family culture, looking after customers, being different through innovation, rewarding, recognizing and empowering and having fun.

Yet Rupa didn't always plan to work at Day Lewis, having initially decided to become a dentist. But once she swapped the dental chair for a seat on the family board she never looked back. So how has she managed the potential conflicts that can arise in a family business? The key is having ground rules, she says:

I have several bosses. My two brothers are effectively my bosses as well. So we have performance reviews quarterly and we live and breathe our management philosophy the same way we expect our managers to do. We have feedback sessions. We've also got ground rules. The three of us are really different in how we manage and how we think, so we've got some common ground rules we created very soon after my father passed away. We had a business coach who helped us develop these ground rules on how to respond to each other and how to work effectively as a team. And now we live by these ground rules and we share them with our managers. Then they use them too, as they are simple concepts that we put together to get the best out of each other, knowing that you're all very different.

These rules include:

- Respond to each other in a timely manner.
- Always respect each other's opinions.
- Avoid talking over each other in larger group meetings.
- Respect people's decisions.
- Have a no-blame culture and learn from our mistakes.
- Invest in ourselves and develop each other.
- Always put the values of a business first and drop our egos.

The latter point is especially important when it comes to how managers deliver value to Day Lewis, Rupa says:

Managers need to drop the ego. They need to be able to understand that everyone is different. This means being more transparent today and being able to manage your team individually. And because everybody's needs are just so different, managers need to be flexible. They also need to understand their strengths but also where they may need support and development. There will always be someone in the organization who can plug your weaknesses.

Other traits Rupa looks for in managers are compassion, empathy and being able to motivate others:

If you call your colleagues family, you must be with them through the hard times as well. So, for me, encouraging vulnerability is key. But colleagues can only do that if they can see their manager showing vulnerability. Bring yourself to work as well. Everybody has a life outside work. Work/life balance doesn't mean you work and then you have your life. It's all mixed together in many circumstances. Work/ life balance became blurred for people who were working from home during the pandemic, for example. So, get to know your colleagues and allow them to get to know you personally as well.

Courage is also important and that can manifest itself in different ways. Quite often it is managers knowing that they don't always have to have the answer and saying, 'I don't know the answer but it's a fantastic question and you've spurred me on to go and find out why that decision was made or what we can do about this.' So put your hand up when you don't know the answer. I own the business and I'm telling you now, I still don't know the answers for half the decisions that have been made and historic things that have happened in our business.

Rather than cascade communication and orders down from an ivory tower head office, Day Lewis flips it the other way, seeing the role of managers as one of supporting the frontline workers and providing information upwards on what is going on at the sharp end, how the directors can help improve the situation or provide better resources. 'I see our managers as my ambassadors,' Rupa says. This is also replicated with the senior leadership team. Managers need to see their managers in the pharmacies, so Rupa and the directors visit as many as they can each year on what they call 'family visits'. 'We go and meet the family to check in on them, ask if they're doing okay, how they are feeling. And we encourage our support colleagues to do the same, whether it's to experience a service that the pharmacy might be offering such as getting a flu jab or just popping in to meet the team and getting a feel of what it's like.' There are also more structured 'back to the floor days' where directors and support colleagues work in the pharmacies. These initiatives all ensure colleagues at every level never stop learning.

It's a mantra Rupa herself follows, being, in her words, a 'fitness/ mindfulness geek' and having recently climbed Mount Kilimanjaro. Therein is a valuable lesson for world-class managers. Don't stop growing and always reach for the heights.

TIP
Rupa's three tips for being a world-class manager

1. Never stop learning

Keep developing your skills – both in areas you already know but also perhaps in those that you may not think are useful at the time but will be going forward. So, keep fresh and keep developing yourself.

2. Build a strong network of support around you

This may be your friends, your contacts or your colleagues. Having strong relationships and a strong network helps you deal with the range of issues you face as a manager and leader.

3. Invest in yourself

Develop yourself. Get to know what you are good at, what relevant areas are for you and feel comfortable acknowledging these. You can't be excellent at everything, so build on your strengths.

16
How to become a strategic leader

Introduction

Developing a strategic mindset is one of the most valuable things we can do, not only to advance ourselves but to advance the performance of the team, the department and the organization overall. This is something I see world-class managers do all the time. They essentially think like the 'board' would. This marks them out from the typical manager who may be more reactive and, while possibly excelling at dealing with the issues and activities required from the organization on a day-to-day basis, may not have the skills to influence and inspire people to look at the bigger picture.

Back in 2013 Management Research Group completed a large global study into the leadership practices and effectiveness of 60,000 managers and executives in more than 140 countries. It found that a strategic approach to leadership was, on average, 10 times more important to the perception of effectiveness than other behaviours studied. In an article in *Harvard Business Review* examining the research, Robert Kabacoff says this was twice as important as the second highest-rated behaviour – communication – and almost 50 times more important than hands-on tactical behaviours.[1]

When the company ran a follow-up study, it asked leaders what leadership behaviours were most critical to their organization's future success. A whopping 97 per cent said strategic leadership.

Our own research with managers found positive signs that they are thinking strategically. Two-thirds say they and their team think strategically and are aligned with the organization, while 81 per cent think there is product delivery or services that could be improved to enable the strategy to be delivered. However, only 46.7 per cent say they have a good understanding of their organization's finances.

So, what do we mean by strategic? There is much literature on the subject, and it can appear somewhat mind blowing. I like to think about it in this way. Your journey goes from point A to point B. How are you going to get there? The 'how' is just your strategy, it's no more complicated than that. Our journey from point A to point B (improving service, for example) means we have to do some things differently, get different support, build new skills, share better information and so on. That's our strategy. Simple.

To start to think strategically, it is useful to put yourself in the shoes of your board members and executive team. These people represent the key disciplines that are useful for any team. Your journey to be a truly world-class manager and to progress rapidly through your organization will rest heavily on your ability to see the world, your business and your team through these multiple lenses of perspective.

So, I'm taking a different perspective in this last chapter by highlighting the core board and senior leadership team roles and what they do. Then I pose some questions for you to think about in order to improve your strategic mindset.

1. Chief financial officer

The chief financial officer (CFO) makes key decisions about costs and investments. They understand that most decisions in organizations involve finance or resources, and they will be concerned with how to best leverage what they have for the good of the enterprise.

What can you do?

Try to get an understanding of the finances of the business. A good place to start is to get a basic knowledge of how to read a balance sheet, income statement and profit and loss account. It will also help to look at how the costs and actions of your team impact on the commercial performance of the department and of the business itself – and of course to see what you can do to make a difference there.

2. Marketing director, or chief marketing officer

The key function of the marketing director or chief marketing officer (CMO) is to look at how best to tell the world about the amazing products or services your organization has to offer. This discipline has an impact both externally and internally. If you were the CMO, how would you talk differently about the value your own team adds to the business?

What can you do?

If you're involved in selling or providing a product or service to customers, it would be good to understand the key messages you're using. Do they match the company ones? Your team is often the one that knows what dealing with customers is like and what receives a favourable response from them. If your customers are internal, think about the brand of your team. What would your customer say about your brand?

3. Operations director, or chief operating officer

This role is focused on making everything work as it should and that the operation runs as it should in order to deliver the right product or service in line with the purpose of the organization. How might a chief operating officer (COO) look differently at the way your operation works? Would they change anything?

What can you do?

Look at how your operation works in reality, not how people think it works. If you analysed it objectively, what would you change? What would you improve? Imagine someone else was looking at how your team operates. What would they suggest?

4. Human resources director, or chief human resources officer

Your HR director is focused on leveraging the investments made in people. Your organization, large or small, will spend a significant amount of its finances on people – finding them, developing them, paying them and so on. So how can you get the biggest bang for your buck from your people? Do they need more support or more challenges to achieve their potential – for the business and for themselves?

What can you do?

Knowing your people well gives you the best chance to get the best possible performance from them. Most people in organizations feel they have skills that aren't adequately being utilized. What skills might your people possess that are not currently being used?

Human capital or human resource is basically the people who cost the organization money, and we want to make sure we maximize the investment we make. Understanding our people and their strengths is key to this.

5. Commercial director, or chief commercial officer

The focus for the CCO is to make sure the business works well, the right deals with suppliers are made and they may be focused on sales too. Again, if you were the CCO of your business, what would you tighten up? Are there any supplier deals that you think need to be better? Is there something that we should change in how we deliver products or services to our customers or key partners?

What can you do?

We'd urge you to see how your organization can be smarter when it comes to its commerciality. This could be as straightforward as knowing who your key competitors are and finding out what they're up to. If you serve internal teams or customers, what's the nature of your service level agreements? Do they need to be revisited to ensure you are getting the best from your team?

6. Head of strategy, or chief strategy officer

This person is the key when it comes to getting the organization from A to B. They will look at the sequence of steps needed to arrive at point B.

What can you do?

The chief strategy officer loves it when everyone understands the strategy and knows what it means for them. Yet most senior managers/leaders don't explain the strategy and share it properly. Understanding what the strategy of your organization is and translating it for your people is a win for you and the CEO.

7. Chief executive officer

Most chief executive officers (CEOs) tell us they have three key jobs. First, making sure there is a clear strategic plan and vision. Second, making sure everyone understands these. And third, making sure they remove any barriers preventing the vision and plan being executed.

What can you do?

World-class managers can learn much from the CEO's three jobs. These are actions we can apply in our teams as well. Visions are important, as we have already seen. They give any team, large or small, something in common, something to work towards and something to believe in. Creating a compelling vision for your team or articulating what you want your team to be famous for is a core skill of world-class managers. You then need to make sure your people understand your vision and help them work out what it means for them.

If you can tie your vision into the organization's vision, then you will be your CEO's best friend!

8. Chairperson

The chairperson of the board is the wise old owl of the organization. They guide and mentor the CEO when needed. They usually have much experience in their field.

What can you do?

Find yourself your own chairman! This may sound odd if you are a small team, but a good mentor is worth their weight in gold. Age isn't the issue here. You may benefit from a young person who can help you with new technology, for example. The key is someone who can help to guide you and your team and who can act as the 'voice of reason'.

9. Chief employee experience officer

This newer role is about looking at the experience of the team in the way that people have looked at the experience of the customer for decades. Successful modern businesses like Airbnb and LinkedIn have put people in these key positions. It's a practical way to make sure we're really thinking through how our people experience work, day to day, which is what has the biggest effect on morale and financial performance.

What can you do?

Take some time and imagine 'a month in the life of' your people. What does coming to work feel like for them? What could be improved? What frustrates them? What works well? Answering these questions will help you to improve how it feels to come to work, improve engagement, impact service delivery and impact that all-important profit.

10. Chief information, or chief technology officer

This is the person ensuring that technology is a real enabler of success and that the organization has the digital capability it needs to win, given its strategy and plans.

What can you do?

Every day, it seems, a new app emerges that holds the promise to help us connect, improve productivity and improve efficiency. Making sure you are on top of technology that can help your teams win is important if you are to be a world-class manager. We've often found that many in-house technology teams have great technology available which many employees are unaware of. So, build a relationship with your technology team and see what may be there to help you. Also, think about how you could help your IT teams to better understand what support you and your team need to be even more successful.

Conclusion

This list is certainly not exhaustive and in some organizations there are lots of variations related to these titles. So, find out what roles are represented on your respective boards and begin to apply these roles to the challenges of your team.

Of course, you can be doing a great job as a standard manager – and there is nothing wrong with that. Ensuring your team completes their tasks effectively to deliver to the bottom line is the hygiene factor of management. Without the ability to do that, you won't even get on to the radar of those above you.

But if you start looking at things strategically, if you think about the future and your people rather than just today and the numbers, imagine how much more success you could have. Inspiring and empowering your people to always deliver their best is a surefire way to be on the path to becoming a world-class manager.

Note

1 Kabacoff, R (2014) Develop Strategic Thinkers Throughout Your Organization, *Harvard Business Review*. hbr.org/2014/02/develop-strategic-thinkers-throughout-your-organization (archived at perma.cc/4G6V-2WEV)

CONCLUSION

I spend around 80 per cent of my time working with CEOs and leaders of organizations from practically every shape and size of company around the world, from stock-market-listed companies to government organizations, charities, NGOs and everything in between. My team and I are asked to advise on 'how to' help to build the capability and indeed capacity of managers to cope with the blisteringly fast rate of change and ever-increasing demands that are placed on their time, energy and attention.

The other 20 per cent of my time is spent talking with audiences, in person and virtually, to everyone from company leaders to undergrads as a part of my desire to prepare young leaders for the challenges that await them. I wish I had had the insights from this book at the beginning of my journey into the world of management, that's for sure!

The big question that I'm asked, all the time, by those with a little experience and those with lots of experience, is the classic nature/nurture question. 'Wayne, tell me, are great leaders/managers born or made?' It's a tough question, which I will answer in a minute, but it's one I want to address as we reach the end of this book.

People ask the question for several reasons. Some ask because they already have a definitive and concrete answer, which for the most part is based on their lived experience of bad management, which they've often been on receiving end of. Their experience has shown them that leopards can't change their spots, that great managers are born with some sort of gift because the managers they've encountered wouldn't do much of what we've talked about in this book. They're certain about this and to a certain extent you can't argue with it, as our experiences are personal, subjective and as real as it gets.

Some ask the question because they've tried to be a better manager; for a while at least, they've organized some better one-to-ones, they've really thought about improving their team communications, they've tried to manage their stakeholders better and they may have concluded that it just isn't for them. So great management must be a cosmic gift of some sort because they've not been able to achieve it.

Then there are those who don't want to bother doing anything different; yes, they've been on the courses, they've read the books, they've probably even advised others on how to do it, but they've never been willing to put in the work, certainly not the prolonged period and volume of work that mastering anything requires. The easy way out is to conclude that it's some sort of gene that skipped them, so they may as well shrug their shoulders and say it's nature, just bad luck they didn't get the 'manager gene'.

Then are those who are serious about it, those whom we've come across from New Zealand to Brazil, from Morocco to Mongolia, who intuitively know that it's possible to be better, to better connect, to get the best from others and themselves. They often ask me this question with a humility that indicates they know that 'nature' just isn't, with all the infinite variables that life throws at us, logical. They know it's about 'what you do', 'what works', they know it's about learning 'how to' and they often want assurance that they're on the right path and to just to keep going.

I guess I've given away my position on nature vs nurture! After meeting with thousands of leaders and tens of thousands of managers, I'm 100 per cent in the nurture camp. This book, this entire series of practical how-tos, tools, approaches, ways, exercises, expert insights, has all been learnt from observing those who've worked hard at it, not by observing those who've been ordained with some divine management wisdom.

Being a great manager is pretty much about the same as being great at anything else; except in the business of emotional engagement, it can 'feel' lousy when either you or someone else gets it wrong. But lousy is just part of the process and I've learnt that the process, if you follow what the great managers 'do', works well.

Someone said to me, on the question 'Is management an art or a science', that if management was indeed a science, then surely by this point, being that we've been at it for thousands of years, there would surely be an equation or algorithm for it by now! It's an art for sure and every great manager you meet has spent years perfecting their art of 'how to' do it.

Part of this art is about what I'd call your 'set-play pieces', which is much of what I wanted to get across to you in this book, from how you actively engage your key stakeholders, to how you run your meetings, to how you make people feel when they emerge from a one-to-one with you. All are set-play pieces that we can certainly all perfect over time if we work at it.

This leads me to my final tip. Everything costs time, but as a busy manager or indeed aspiring manager, you will most likely have no time. So, here's the tip: pick a date in the future where your diary begins to look a little less busy (this could be in three to six months' time) and block out 5 to 10 per cent of your week. And keep that time sacrosanct. How would I suggest you spend this time? On yourself of course, spend it on evaluating your impact on those around you, your team, your business, your customers, your shareholders, your stakeholders. As busy managers we've hardly any time to think and to evaluate our impact.

Working this 5 to 10 per cent of your time into your natural operating 'rhythm' is a smart way to make sure you're always focused on how to become a world-class manager. In truth, the journey never ends, so I hope this book will help you to better enjoy it.

INDEX

The index is filed in alphabetical, word-by-word order. Acronyms are filed as presented. Numbers are filed as spelt out. Locators in italics denote information within figures or tables, those in roman numerals denote information within the preface.

CPSIA information can be obtained
at www.ICGtesting.com
Printed in the USA
JSHW071508230223
38141JS00007B/37